IN CHRIST'S IMAGE TRAINING

LEVEL I
TRACK FOUR

UNITY

TAKEN FROM WRITINGS BY

PASTOR FRANCIS FRANGIPANE

UNITY

In Christ's Image Training
125 Robins Square Ct
Robins, IA 52328
Phone: 1-319-395-7617
Fax: 1-319-395-7353
Web: www.ICITC.org

Published by
Arrow Publications Inc.
P.O. Box 10102
Cedar Rapids, IA 52410
Phone: 1-319-395-7833
Fax: 1-319-395-7353
Web: www.ArrowBookstore.com

CONTENTS

TRACK FOUR: UNITY

INTRODUCTION

Even aged men believe that, in their lifetimes, they will see the return of Jesus Christ. Since the end of WWII and the restoration of Israel in 1948, the heavens have been saturated with the fulfillment of prophetic Scripture. Indeed, not since the first century have more prophecies come to pass. Beloved, we must conclude that the spiritual season in which we find ourselves is the beginning of the fullness of times, the period leading up to the return of Christ.

Yet, although most Christians agree that we live in prophetic times, two specific tasks remain unfulfilled: the evangelization of the nations and the restoration of purity and unity in the born-again church (see Matt 24:12; Rev 19, Eph 5). These two are interrelated, for it is the purified church, united and filled with love for Jesus, that shall turn the nations to God.

We have given ourselves to the process of purification in our first three manuals. In this study we shall consider unity. Many Christians believe that we must have an outpouring of the Holy Spirit before we will find true unity. Let me remind you, beloved, the disciples, both men and women, were all of one mind before Pentecost (see Acts 1:14). If there had not been unity among the disciples prior to Pentecost, there would not have been an outpouring of the Holy Spirit on Pentecost. The outpouring did not create unity; unity made the way for the outpouring. Unity is just as essential today if we will see the great outpouring of the Holy Spirit repeated in our world.

In our previous three manuals, we set our goal to personally attain the nature of Christ. We are not talking about attaining a religion about Jesus; we are in pursuit of the life of Jesus. Yet, we recognize that we cannot take a step toward attaining Christlikeness without embracing humility. To be able to revel in meekness as a way of life; to gain the capacity to not only see where we are wrong, but to humble ourselves and confess our errors, is to truly make spiritual progress.

While humility opens our eyes to perceive our need, prayer enables us to appropriate God's answer. The very moment we look to God in prayer, spiritual power begins to awaken in our lives. The fact that God Himself is humble, that He is actually entreated by our prayers, reveals that the future is not irreversibly clocked. Redemptive intercession, allied with divine intervention, can transform the world around us. In fact, we learned that our perfection *requires* we live in an imperfect world, for it is here where true Christlikeness matures. Indeed, an imperfect world is "job security" for an intercessor.

If we look at the DNA of the early disciples, we see that they were devoted to Jesus and His teachings, they were humble, and they were devoted to intercessory prayer. The result was their Christ-centered unity became a landing strip for the outpouring of the Holy Spirit.

Let me add one more thought about the value of unity. Psalm 133 reveals that, where brethren dwell together in unity, God commands His eternal blessing. The unity God seeks is a deep thing. Satan seeks to exploit our differences; God seeks to tune us with each other and harmonize our calling until we corporately represent Christ. Thus, we need brethren of differing temperaments and specialized callings; our unity must transcend the culture boundaries of race or wealth to where we truly love, respect and enjoy one another. The by-product of such a life is that God can use us to reach a variety of people in our society.

Psalm 133 compares the effect of spiritual unity to the oil that came upon Aaron's head and flowed down his beard, ultimately reaching to the edges of his garment. The oil identified here was the precious holy oil that only the priest received just prior to entering the presence of the Living God. Everyone else outside the holy of holies served the Almighty through rules and ritual. The priest, with this fragrant oil covering him, actually entered the reality of God Himself. True spiritual unity literally opens heaven to us.

Yet our quest for unity will remain an unattainable goal without the establishment in our lives of the first three values discussed in manuals one through three. Unity is the fragrance that arises from humble, prayerful, Christ-centered people. It enables us to become the habitation of God.

In this study, we will look at unity and also study the root and effects of division. Beloved, this manual contains the prerequisites needed to bring healing to families, churches and cities. Healthy families and healthy churches are what bring lasting transformation to cities and nations.

SESSION ONE:

THE ROOTS OF DIVISION

CHAPTER ONE

THE GREAT DIVISION

Lucifer's terrible crime was not only that he rebelled against God, as evil as that was. Worse, through slander against God and deception, he stole away a third of the angels as well. Though banished to hell, Lucifer's war against the Almighty continues. Indeed, every time he divides another church, part of his goal is to strike again the heart of God.

If you have ever been through a church split, you are all too familiar with the terrible churning of emotions and the inconsolable distress that accompanies this descent into hell. If you are unfamiliar with the experience, expect that large factions of otherwise nice Christians will be pitted against one another. They will participate in slander, anger, deception, fear, bitterness, hatred, gossip, unforgiveness, strife, rebellion and pride.

Any of these attitudes, isolated in a single individual, would be recognized and exposed as sin. However, when they occur en masse in a church split, they are somehow considered righteous. Anger is redefined as "fighting for a principle." Slander and gossip now enlist as allies "in search of the truth."

The epicenter of the split may have been localized in a single church, but the shockwaves are felt across the area-wide body of Christ. News of the conflict is communicated in whispered tones, like when hearing of a family member who has a serious cancer. And it is a cancer—a split is a malignant life system, a false growth that is empowered by anger, pride and ambition instead of the meekness and patience of Christ.

Citywide church leaders shake their heads and sigh. Even if they barely knew the troubled church, they suffer sympathy pains. They are concerned. Those who have experienced the heartache of their own split also shudder, as they remember the still unresolved conflict they carry regarding those who divided their church. Still other pastoral leaders become restless and more guarded over their flocks, wary lest the spirit of strife infiltrate their churches as well.

Additionally, the evangelists of the city know that, at least for a season, it will be harder to win the lost. Indeed, as rumors and details of the split reach the ears of the unsaved, the pettiness and politics that accompany a split remind the unbelieving world of why they are keeping their distance from church.

I have traveled throughout most of the Christian world speaking to pastors and church leaders. It is my experience that, while divisions are found everywhere, splits are more frequent and often more mean-spirited in America. Is it our fierce love of independence and freedom? Or is it because of our more aggressive cultural nature? Regardless, American splits tend to have the least civility.

The reasons for church splits are many. Divisions may originate from confusion concerning church governments. To whom has God really given final authority in any given congregation? Sometimes, the root of conflict is simply misguided ambition in one or more associate leaders. And, of course, there is always the issue of spiritual warfare. Often, just as a church begins an upward swing in attendance or spiritual growth, demonically manipulated strife emerges. So, we must ask ourselves: When we see a serious division in a church, are we really looking at the work of the same kind of spirit that manipulated Absalom, Korah or Jezebel?

Perhaps splits involve some combination of all of the above. Yet, regardless of the unique source of each division, Jesus warned that when our house is divided, it "shall not stand" (Matt 12:25). Clearly, when a division strikes a church, its impact is felt throughout the community. It is a war in which the devil is the only one who wins.

HEARTACHE IN HEAVEN

We may think the Lord is personally unfamiliar with the pain of a church split. He is not. In fact, church leaders can take some comfort that God Himself, even in all His perfection, suffered a type of split. You may recall that, before the creation of man, heaven endured a time of great rebellion, a "split," if you will.

In those days Satan was known as Lucifer, or "Hillel Ben Shahar" in the Hebrew language. The name *Hillel* came from the root word, *Hallel,* which means "to praise, worship, adore"; *Ben Shahar* meant "son of the dawn." The implication is that Lucifer was the chief worship leader at the dawn of creation. Endowed with the gifts of leadership and creativity in music, his position was not enough for him. Fueled by jealousy and ambition, Lucifer led a third of the angels to rebel against the authority of God.

Consider the cunning of Lucifer, our ancient foe. He was able to actually convince angels, who were gazing upon the resplendent glory of God, that they could win a war against their Creator! In privileged awe they had seen galaxies emerge from the mouth of God. Yet somehow they came to believe that, under Lucifer's leadership, they could defeat the Almighty.

They knew God was fully cognizant of their every thought, yet they believed they could out-think Him. Through stealth, slander and seduction, Lucifer engendered discontentment among the angels so that the very pleasures of heaven could not satisfy them. He then lured them from the un-imaginable splendor of God's presence, convinc-ing them the unfathomable outer darkness was more suited for their cause. Yes, consider the de-ceptive powers of our ancient foe and wonder not that he could separate good friends in a church split here on earth.

How long the rebellion in heaven lasted, we do not know. Or what deception Lucifer spun, it is not written. The Bible only grants fleeting re-flections into that horrible, cataclysmic divide. Still, one wonders: Did the Lord remain unaffected by the strife? Was the Heavenly Father perfectly aloof from the pain of separation or did He suffer heart-ache when those whom He gave the gift of life rebelled against Him? Remember, God watched the great lie spread, infecting one angel after an-other, until a full third joined in the insurrection. Was this division the first great pain in the heart of God?

Beloved, consider also with trembling fear: Un-til Lucifer rebelled against God, to our knowledge, hell did not exist. Hell became a reality as a conse-quence of division.

In subsequent chapters we will look at some of the causes as well as some cures for divisions and splits. We will discuss kingdom protocols and expose how the enemy can manipulate our reli-gious ambitions. For now, it is enough that we ac-knowledge that division and splits are serious sins. They remind God of when hell began.

Let's pray: *Lord, forgive us for tolerating this terrible sin. Master, we know that our division is a blight upon Your people. Cleanse us of the effects of division and empower each of us with grace to bring unity to Your church. In Jesus' name. Amen.*

—FROM THE BOOK, *IT'S TIME TO END CHURCH SPLITS*

SELF TEST, CHAPTER ONE

Remember, we are looking for answers that correspond with this training. Please write out your essay answers, allowing the Holy Spirit to provoke your thoughts. You may want to use them for group discussion. Note: we do not provide answers to essay questions. To check your multiple choice answers, see answer key in the next session.

Chapter 1, Essay #1: In two paragraphs, describe the sad similarities between Lucifer's rebellion and a church split.

Chapter 1, Essay #2: What are some of the ripple effects caused by a church split?

1. During a church split, large factions of otherwise nice Christians participate in:
    a. slander, anger, deception, and fear
    b. bitterness, hatred and gossip
    c. unforgiveness, strife, rebellion and pride
    d. all the above

2. In the midst of a church split:
    a. everyone is Christlike
    b. anger is redefined as "fighting for a principle"
    c. slander and gossip now enlist as allies "in search of the truth"
    d. both b & c

3. During division in a church, evangelists know:
    a. that rumors and details of the split reach the unsaved
    b. thousands of souls will be saved
    c. it will be harder to win the lost for a season
    d. both a & c

4. Jesus warned (Matt 12:25) that a house divided:
    a. makes two sound houses
    b. is multiplication
    c. shall not stand
    d. is predicted

5. Endowed with gifts of leadership, Lucifer's position was not enough for him; he rebelled and led:
   a. many to truth
   b. 1/3 of the angels to rebel against the authority of God
   c. 1/4 of the angels to rebel against the authority of God
   d. no one who hadn't already chosen to follow elsewhere

6. When we consider the deceptive powers of our ancient foe, Lucifer, we clearly see that he can:
   a. slay the dragon
   b. do a little bit of good
   c. separate good friends in a church split
   d. discern and communicate truth

7. Consider with trembling fear, until Lucifer rebelled against God, to our knowledge:
   a. worship did not exist
   b. hell did not exist
   c. free will did not exist
   d. all the above

CHAPTER TWO

LUCIFER'S NATURE: AMBITION

No virtue manifests in our lives without Satan awakening a corresponding vice: Traveling with obedience is pride, and just behind faith walks presumption. Yes, and walking in the shadow of godly vision, ambition follows.

There are perhaps many sources of strife that lead to divisions and splits, but none are more subtle nor powerful than religious ambition. This is especially so when a subordinate leader begins to imagine God has called them to take the place of a senior leader or department head.

As we again reflect back to the first great division, through the prophet Isaiah the Holy Spirit gives us insight into the motive of Lucifer's rebellion against divine authority: selfish ambition. This revelation of Lucifer's ambition manifests succinctly through the voice of the Babylonian king mentioned in Isaiah 14 (actually identified as "Lucifer" in the King James Bible). Listen to the edict of God against the unholy objectives of the prince of darkness:

> How you are fallen from heaven, O Lucifer, son of the morning! How you are cut down to the ground, you who weakened the nations! For you have said in your

heart: "I will ascend into heaven; I will exalt my throne above the stars of God; I will also sit on the mount of the congregation on the farthest sides of the north; I will ascend above the heights of the clouds; I will be like the Most High."
—Isaiah 14:12–14 NKJV

A number of Bible commentators agree that this quote, though ascribed to a man, actually embodies Lucifer's unrestrained lust for preeminence and position. Five times the focus of Lucifer's pride speaks through the king's great ambition, "I will," until he states plainly his unholy quest to supplant God as the supreme being worshipped on planet earth.

Lucifer not only desires to be like God, but he seeks to "ascend to heaven" and establish his throne above the stars of God, which is where the Almighty sits! The Revelation of John confirms this goal repeatedly throughout the book: Satan seeks to be worshipped. He seeks the place of God in heaven and he seeks the place of God in us.

This is vital for our discernment: *Satan is primarily a religious spirit.* He does not want to destroy the world; he wants to rule it. He led a third of the angels against God's authority in heaven, and he manipulates religious ambition in subordinate leaders to usurp God's delegated authority in His church on earth.

Of course, Lucifer's involvement in the religion of man is widespread and multifaceted, but nothing he does is more subtle or diabolical than when he deceives good Christians to turn against their own church leaders. Astutely, Jesus warned that a "house divided against itself shall not stand" (Matt 12:25).

Listen well, it is right to aspire to the office of an overseer; it is wrong to be ambitious for the office of your overseer. It is honorable to desire a church to serve as shepherd; it is hellish to engender discontent against the leader of your current church so you can take his place.

Because a subordinate leader cannot simply take the place of the senior leader through physical force, he must work covertly. He has to make himself appear righteous and find ways to make the senior leader appear unrighteous, or at least not as righteous or wise as the subordinate postures himself to be. The one in rebellion always has an issue; there is always something not right—and if he were in charge, he would do all things better. Reasonable communication or compromise on problems which are not serious sin issues will never remedy the conflict, because the subordinate does not want compromise; he desires control. As Lucifer seeks to take the place of God, so the subordinate covets the pastor's position.

Whenever we seek to take the place of another whom God has placed in authority, we are conforming ourselves to the image of Lucifer, not Christ.

GODLY VISION, FLESHLY MOTIVES

The deception surrounding ambition is especially powerful when someone actually has a vision from God but seeks to fulfill it in the flesh. Early in my spiritual journey, the Lord gave me a vision about my future. It was an exciting promise, alive with the glory and power of God, bursting with hope to reach nations for Christ. However, other than focusing me on the presence of the Lord, the vision came without any specifics as to when or how it would be fulfilled.

In those days, I thought the Lord's promise was the same as His command, something I had to fulfill in whatever way I could. Indeed, because of my spiritual immaturity, I could find no reason why the Lord's promise should not be fulfilled quickly (when one is immature, he does not realize he is immature, because he is immature.)

According to my imagination, it would be easy for God to fulfill His promise, and I had a preponderance of ideas to help Him. Young as I was spiritually, I was simply unfamiliar with the Holy Spirit's work of preparation: the call to die to self, the seasons of learning patience and maintaining vision through testing—all of which needed to occur before the vision from the Almighty would draw near to fulfillment.

A true word from God will test you before it fulfills you. Consider Joseph. The Scripture says, "Until the time that his word came to pass, the word of the Lord tested him" (Ps 105:19). The longer my spiritual fulfillment delayed, the more my character was being forced to change. With great passion I wanted my destiny to unfold; I just did not want God's discipline. With unrelenting hope, I desired the crown God set before me; I just didn't see the cross that stood between the Father's initial promise and my spiritual fulfillment.

I have come to believe that it is probably impossible to gain spiritual advancement without ambition rising within us. In and of itself, I don't even think ambition is blatantly wrong as long as our zeal is guarded by humility and submission. To have ambition, yet be able to wait, trust God, and put others first means the Holy Spirit rules our lives, and thus transforms ambition into patient obedience. It is when ambition and pride unite that we become spiritually dangerous.

But let me say, even if our motives are not perfect, we need to persist with our destiny. Don't become so introspective that you stop walking forward. There are many times, especially in our early years, when we must persevere in spite of our pride and fleshly motives. Ask God to correct you as you move forward; don't be afraid to take faith and step out. However, let us be aware of those times when our zeal is creating strife and confusion around us. For when we are causing strife, we are moving away from our destiny, not toward it.

Ambition might arise as a consequence of faith, but it is not faith. Ambition is the attempt of the flesh to fulfill the promise of the Spirit. In my inner person, I considered my ambition to be a virtue; I was actually proud of it. Abraham had it when, in his impatience, it caused him and Hagar to produce Ishmael. Ultimately, the Lord said of Ishmael, "He will be a wild donkey of a man, his hand will be against everyone, and everyone's hand will be against him" (Gen 16:12). In other words, he would be a constant source of strife. Ambition, when driving us to move ahead of the Lord's timing, will almost always produce strife in those around us.

True faith, however, rests in God's integrity and faithfulness. A person of faith can entrust his calling and gifts to the timing and wisdom of God. Thus, true faith rests in God, even when what is promised is not yet seen. It does not strive; it trusts. Abraham's faith outgrew his ambition because he learned to trust that the Lord was faithful (see Heb 10:23). He became "fully assured that what [God] had promised, He was able also to perform" (Rom 4:21).

The ambitious soul, however, fails to trust God for the timing and opening of appropriate doors; it spawns impatience and striving to fulfill one's destiny. Ambition tries to create doors where none exist.

The Bible tells us plainly that none of those whom God used were able to avoid an extended time of preparation. God's call and His timing are the work of His hands. Our task is to remain faithful to the place He has us in and to maintain integrity in support of others.

Ambition creates strife, in part, because it is rooted in fear. This fear brings striving and jealousy into the Christian's soul, especially as others occupy positions we deem necessary for our fulfillment. Because we do not truly know the Lord in the way of patience and trust, the voice we most often obey is not God's, but the urgency of our own ambition.

Consequently, James tells us, "Where jealousy and selfish ambition exist," there will inevitably emerge "disorder and every evil thing" (James 3:16). Disorder comes as people violate proper protocols for spiritual advancement and begin to criticize those in a position over or alongside them. Disorder opens the door for "every evil thing" to enter, as attention is drawn away from the pastor's God-appointed responsibilities and given to lengthy, usually fruitless, meetings spent trying to remedy strife.

Ambition is obsessed with fulfillment. When rebuked, though it puts on the face of the penitent, it grows angrier because of the new delay. There is only one remedy for religious ambition: it must die.

THE PATH TO LEADERSHIP

If you are a subordinate leader and desire your own church, do not find fault with your current leader as a means of seeking advancement. The answer to your success is unveiled in Psalm 37. Here David revealed the attitude that ultimately promoted him to kingship. Remember, David was submitted to King Saul, an unjust king driven by fits of madness. Still, David wrote,

> Trust in the Lord, and do good; dwell in the land and cultivate faithfulness. Delight yourself in the Lord; and He will give you the desires of your heart. Commit your way to the Lord, trust also in Him, and He will do it. And He will bring forth your righteousness as the light, and your judgment as the noonday. Rest in the Lord and wait patiently for Him; do not fret because of him who prospers in his way, because

of the man who carries out wicked schemes. Cease from anger, and forsake wrath; do not fret, it leads only to evildoing.   —Psalm 37:3–8

Even though in my earlier years I wrestled with my own ambitions of spiritual fulfillment, I never sought the place of another leader. I learned to trust in the Lord and do good. I saw that fretting over what was wrong in those around me only led to evil doing. Let us, therefore, cease from anger and forsake wrath. Let us delight ourselves in the Lord and He will give us the desires of our hearts at the proper time.

Let's pray: *Lord Jesus, forgive me for my selfish motives and unbroken will. I confess there have been times when my pride and ambition have generated strife. I have been so blind to this. Help me to serve You with my whole heart and let You promote me at the proper time. For Your glory, I pray. Amen.*

—FROM THE BOOK, *IT'S TIME TO END CHURCH SPLITS*

SELF TEST, CHAPTER TWO

Remember, we are looking for answers that correspond with this training. Please write out your essay answers, allowing the Holy Spirit to provoke your thoughts. You may want to use them for group discussion. Note: we do not provide answers to essay questions. To check your multiple choice answers, see answer key in the next session.

Chapter 2, Essay #1: What can some of the manifestations be when religious ambition occurs?

Chapter 2, Essay #2: What are some of Satan's vices?

1. There can be many sources of strife that lead to divisions and splits, but none are more subtle nor more powerful than:
    a. religious ambition
    b. denominations joining together
    c. patience and love
    d. Christlikeness

2. No virtue manifests in our lives without Satan awakening _____.
    a. unity, wholeness and integrity

CHAPTER TWO: LUCIFER'S NATURE: AMBITION

b. a corresponding vice (weakness of character)
c. virtues we already have
d. those who know us to see the change

3. It is right to aspire to the office of an overseer, but it is wrong to:
   a. covet a leader's position
   b. be a subordinate
   c. be ambitious for the office of your overseer
   d. both a & c

4. The deception surrounding ambition is especially powerful when someone actually has:
   a. a stronger opinion than their leaders do
   b. a demonic spirit
   c. a vision from God but seeks to fulfill it in the flesh
   d. a really lame idea

5. As we become familiar with the Holy Spirit's work of preparation, what needs to occur in us before our vision from God can be fulfilled?
   a. gaining a higher position of authority
   b. a call to die to self
   c. seasons of learning patience and maintaining vision through testing
   d. both b & c

6. What transforms ambition into patient obedience?
   a. our zeal and passion being guarded by humility and submission
   b. getting the position we've been striving after
   c. to have ambition yet be able to wait, trust God, and put others first
   d. both a & c

7. In times when we need to persevere, to step out in faith in spite of our imperfect motives, what should we be careful of?
   a. not to allow delays to keep us from moving forward in our vision
   b. times when our zeal is creating strife and confusion around us
   c. watch for incorrect expectations of others for us to lay down our vision
   d. all the above

8. What was the attitude David revealed in Psalm 37 that became the pathway to leadership?
   a. trusting and delighting in the Lord
   b. not fretting as others prosper
   c. resting and waiting patiently for the Lord's timing
   d. all the above

QUOTE:

"When one is immature, he does not realize he is immature, because he is immature."

SESSION TWO:

THE POTENTIAL OF UNITY

CHAPTER THREE

THE HOUSE OF GLORY

Lord, we consecrate ourselves as priests unto You; we sanctify ourselves without regard to divisions! Build us together with those who love You as we do! Make us a living temple and then draw all men, even all nations, unto Yourself.

WHEN GLORY FILLED THE TEMPLE

The dedication of Solomon's temple offers us a picture of what God is seeking in the church. The temple was built and, in great pageantry and celebration, it was consecrated to the Lord. Solomon offered a sacrifice of 22,000 oxen and 120,000 sheep. Then, immediately after the king prayed, for the first time in over 400 years, the glory of God was manifested in full view of the people. We read, "Fire came down from heaven and consumed the burnt offering and the sacrifices; and the glory of the Lord filled the house" (2 Chron 7:1). If the Lord would honor the dedication of the physical temple with a visible manifestation of His glory, how much more does He seek to reveal His glorious Presence in His living temple, the church?

But there were prerequisites which occurred prior to this appearance of the Lord. First, it was not until Solomon's temple was actually built, with all its separate aspects connected together and covered in gold, that the glory of the Lord appeared.

Likewise, we also must be built together and "perfected in unity" if we would see the fullness of the Lord displayed among us and the world believe in Christ (see John 17:23). There is no other aspect of life more glorious or wonderful than this.

The next requirement deals with our worship. The Lord was not revealed until the singers, trumpeters and priests lifted their voices in praise and worship to God. We cannot overstate the need to be worshippers of God. Even now, in a number of corporate church services, a faint, luminous glory is appearing, like a living cloud, drawn by the purity of the ascending worship.

However, there was another dimension of preparation which also preceded the revelation of glory and pertains to those in leadership. "And when the priests came forth from the holy place (for all the priests who were present had sanctified themselves, without regard to divisions) . . . then the house, the house of the Lord, was filled with a cloud, so that the priests could not stand to minister because of the cloud . . . for the glory of the Lord filled the house of God" (2 Chron 5:11–14).

Their divisions in the priesthood had been ordained by God according to individual families and unique purposes. Yet, when the priests entered the holy place, they "sanctified themselves, without regard to divisions" (v 11). When it came to building the temple and entering the Holy Place, the priest had to *disregard* the lesser place of service to enter the greater place of divine Presence.

So also today, "without regard to divisions," churches are entering the holy place of Christ's Presence. In cities throughout the world, thousands of church leaders from every denominational or ethnic background are functionally uniting with each other: They are becoming the holy body of

Christ. The outcome? We are being "fitted together . . . growing into a holy temple in the Lord; in whom [we] also are being built together into a dwelling of God in the Spirit" (Eph 2:21–22).

Notice these words: "fitted together . . . built together." The true house of the Lord is only revealed when the church puts away fear and divisions. Only then can we truly become the temple of the Lord, "a dwelling of God in the Spirit."

THE SOURCE OF GLORY

Jesus prayed, "And the glory which Thou hast given Me I have given to them; that they may be one, just as We are one; I in them, and Thou in Me, that they may be perfected in unity" (John 17:22–23). Jesus is not coming to give us a new form of church government or new doctrines and programs. He is coming to be glorified in His saints and marvelled at by all who have believed! (see 2 Thess 1:10) It was for this that He called us, that we may gain His glory! (see 2 Thess 2:14)

Let us each see that God is building something in this hour which will far exceed our current definition of the church. God is building us together into "a holy temple in the Lord," a place where His very glory shall be revealed!

This next prayer is perhaps the most important in this manual. It is our response to God's call to build His house. It is uniquely directed toward those who are church leaders and intercessors, to build "without regard to divisions." If you are a leader, and you see the vision of the house of the Lord, please pray with us.

Let's pray: *Lord Jesus, I thank You for granting me a new opportunity to serve You. I repent of the areas in my heart where I allowed division and self-interest to guide my actions. Jesus, I want to see Your glory, even to abide, as did Moses, in Your sacred Presence. Master, I consecrate my heart, without regard to divisions, to Your sacred service. Before You I sanctify my life and my church to build the house of the Lord in my city. Amen.*

—FROM THE BOOK, THE HOUSE OF THE LORD

SELF TEST, CHAPTER THREE

Remember, we are looking for answers that correspond with this training. Please write out your essay answers, allowing the Holy Spirit to provoke your thoughts. You may want to use them for group discussion. Note: we do not provide answers to essay questions. To check your multiple choice answers, see answer key in the next session.

Chapter 3, Essay #1: What were the prerequisites before the Glory of God was manifested in Solomon's temple?

Chapter 3, Essay #2: What does Jesus say in John 17:22? (great memory verse)

1. The dedication of Solomon's temple offers a picture of:
   a. what church has always been like
   b. the negative effect of large sacrificial offerings
   c. what God is seeking in the church
   d. God's disappointment

2. What is prerequisite to "a revealing of the Lord's Presence" as modeled in the dedication of Solomon's temple?
   a. be built together and "perfected in unity"
   b. need to be worshippers
   c. staying faithful to only one denomination
   d. both a & b

3. What is another dimension of preparation which also preceded the revelation of glory and pertains to those in leadership?
   a. ordination
   b. priests sanctifying themselves "without regard to divisions"
   c. being initiated into a specific doctrinal pattern
   d. receiving scholarly credentials

4. God is building something in this hour which will far exceed our current definition of the church. He is building us together into:
   a. universalism
   b. a place where we can hide from the world
   c. a holy temple in the Lord
   d. an unconsecrated place of refuge

QUOTE:

"Let us each see that God is building something in this hour which will far exceed our current definition of the church. God is building us together into 'a holy temple in the Lord,' a place where His very glory shall be revealed!"

CHAPTER FOUR

IT TAKES A CITYWIDE CHURCH

It is incredible, but many Christians actually believe that the only unity there will be in the last days is in the apostate church. The very spirit they think they are avoiding, the antichrist, is what has divided them from the rest of the church! (see 1 John 2:18–19) It is simply unscriptural and a sin for the believing, citywide church of Jesus Christ not to maintain the unity of the Spirit!

UNITED IN WORSHIP AND WAR

One need not be a biblical scholar to recognize the Jews had to be uncompromisingly united in their worship of God. All Israel was required to come to Jerusalem three times a year to worship during the feasts. If their worship was compromised to where they began to serve the pagan gods of the region, they were quickly defeated in their battles.

However, in addition to unity in worship, they also had to be united in warfare. Unless they embraced their battle as "one man," their victory was rarely assured (see Judges 6:16; 20:1, 8, 11; 1 Sam 11:7; Ezra 3:1; Neh 8:1).

From the beginning, the Lord has desired that we should be our brother's "keeper." Today, He is calling us to cease fighting with one another and to become a family that fights for each other.

There is an Old Testament story which captures the heart we are seeking. The Israelites were in the land of Gilead about to cross the Jordan River. However, the tribes of Reuben and Gad, which had amassed much livestock, asked that their inheritance be given first, as the land on which they stood was suitable for grazing. Their request angered Moses for he assumed they sought to divide from the nation in order to gain their individual inheritance (see Num 32).

Yet, Reuben and Gad had a greater vision than Moses realized. The declaration they made to Moses is the attitude we must have concerning the other churches in our city. Reuben said, "We will build here sheepfolds for our livestock and cities for our little ones; but we ourselves will be armed ready to go before the sons of Israel, until we have brought them to their place" (Num 32:16–17). They refused to put down their swords until there was peace and prosperity for *all* of Israel.

So also for us, we must realize we are all part of the same body. When one congregation is in a battle, we are all in battle. Therefore, the more mature churches should equip their saints for war. Individuals should be trained to protect and defend the rest of the body of Christ in the city. The attitude in Reuben and Gad, "We will not return to our homes until every one of the sons of Israel has possessed his inheritance" (Num 32:18), must become the attitude of the citywide church.

Every assembly should maintain their "sheepfolds" for the sense of family and continuity among them, as well as to provide a place of spiritual shelter, "cities for [their] little ones." However, while doing this, we must keep our swords drawn, ready to fight on behalf of our brethren.

One obstacle we must overcome is due to our inflated sense of ministerial pride, which causes us to think we are, in all things, more spiritual than those in other churches. This deception infects congregations across the board. Consequently, we remain divided, kept in isolation by our own spiritual pride, never discerning that the enemy has the church down the street similarly thinking they are more spiritual than we.

However, as God delivers us all of our arrogance, as we truly become more spiritual, our attitude changes. We see that we are not called to judge other churches but to lay down our lives for them. Indeed, what God is doing today is very much like the period of restoration when the Jews returned from Babylon. In those days, Nehemiah supervised the building of the wall around Jerusalem. He instructed the workers to carry a building tool in one hand and a sword in the other (see Neh 4:17). If one section of the wall came under attack, a trumpet was sounded and all the Jews rallied to defend that area.

So also it must be for us. Many times the enemy has been able to defeat a particular church only because the rest of the local body of Christ was indifferent or unaware of the battle. In this context especially, we must perceive that it takes a citywide church to win the citywide war.

I hear the reply: *The churches in our city are dead and we alone are left.* Such was Elijah's lament, but God assured him there were yet 7,000 who were faithful. Ezekiel also thought he stood alone, but God brought him out to a valley of dry bones and commanded him to prophesy. *After* the bones came together, *then* the Spirit entered and, behold, they were "an exceedingly great army" (Ezek 37:10b).

Today, God has an "exceedingly great army" He is preparing. Through them He intends to pull down the strongholds in their cities. We must be *connected in Christ* before the Spirit will anoint us for effective spiritual warfare. We need prophetic vision to see beyond the apparent deadness of our local churches. We must perceive the army God is raising up in this hour, and embrace anointed intercession born of such vision.

Please hear me. We can have national days of prayer, regional weeks of supplication—we can even call tens of thousands to pray for specific areas to change, but if the church which dwells in that area is bound and divided by strife, the enemy will not be plundered. Whenever we pray against the spiritual forces of wickedness over a region, our first line of offense is praying for the churches to be united in their worship and their warfare. Why pray for the church? If there is "jealousy and selfish ambition" in the church, there will inevitably be "disorder and every evil thing" in that locality (James 3:16).

Therefore, we conclude: It takes a citywide church to win the citywide war. All of our individual evangelistic programs, our Sunday teachings and aggressive attempts to wage spiritual warfare are only of limited value if we remain divided along denominational or racial lines. However, even as one person's transformation from carnality to the image of Christ can revolutionize a church, so the transformation of the citywide church into the image of Christ can revolutionize a city.

Let's pray: *Lord Jesus, You taught that a house divided against itself cannot stand. Yet, we have justified our divisions, using peripheral doctrines to mask our pride and ambition. We repent for thinking more highly of ourselves than we ought. Master, show me creative ways to build up the walls and repair the divisions between other*

Christians and myself, and between other congregations and my own. Amen.

—FROM THE BOOK, *THE HOUSE OF THE LORD*

SELF TEST, CHAPTER FOUR

Remember, we are looking for answers that correspond with this training. Please write out your essay answers, allowing the Holy Spirit to provoke your thoughts. You may want to use them for group discussion. Note: we do not provide answers to essay questions. To check your multiple choice answers, see answer key in the next session.

Chapter 4, Essay #1: What are some Scriptures that indicate we must be united in warfare?

Chapter 4, Essay #2: What are some obstacles that must be overcome in order to become a citywide church?

1. In Bible times, the Jews had to be united in worship; they also had to be:
   a. secretive about their desires for different styles of worship
   b. united in warfare
   c. strong enough to individually conquer in battle
   d. prepared to fight with one another

2. As the Old Testament story of Reuben and Gad demonstrated, the attitude of the citywide church today should also be:
   a. keeping our swords drawn, ready to fight on behalf of our brethren
   b. making sure our own assembly's needs are met and then waiting
   c. not returning to our homes until every one has possessed his inheritance
   d. both a & c

3. Why should every assembly also maintain their "sheepfolds"?
   a. for a time and place to rest and lay down our swords
   b. for the sense of continuity among them
   c. to provide a place of spiritual shelter, "cities for (their) little ones"
   d. both b & c

4. What obstacle or illusion do we need to overcome as a church?
   a. believing our ability to "rightly divide the Word" makes us more spiritual than those in other churches
   b. believing we can really become Christlike
   c. our desire to bring various churches together in prayer
   d. both a & c

5. We are not called to judge other churches, but to:
   a. form an opinion of them that can then guide our prophesy for them
   b. keep our distance if they are different in doctrinal beliefs
   c. lay down our lives for them
   d. both b & c

6. Many times the enemy has been able to defeat a particular church only because:
   a. the rest of the citywide church was indifferent or unaware of the defeated church's battle
   b. they were not worshipping the one true God
   c. their doctrines were incorrect
   d. they were not guarding their own section of the wall

7. Whenever we pray against the spiritual forces of wickedness over a region, our first and most significant line of offense is:
   a. just waiting for the Lord to raise up others
   b. holding more national days of prayer
   c. calling thousands to pray
   d. first praying for the born again churches to be united in their worship and their warfare

8. How can we see beyond the deadness of our local churches if we feel alone in our city?
   a. stop looking around at what other churches are doing
   b. leave your own church and plant yourself in the one you criticize as dead, to pray for them
   c. gain prophetic vision, as in Ezekiel 37, and perceive the army God is raising up
   d. get new glasses

QUOTE:

"It takes a citywide church to win a citywide war."

Session Three:

Enemies of Oneness

SESSION THREE AUDIO MESSAGES:

3a. How to Honor Others
3b. Repairers of the Breach

ANSWER KEY TO LAST SESSION'S
SELF TEST QUESTIONS:

CHAPTER THREE. The House of Glory
1.c, 2.d, 3.b, 4.c.
CHAPTER FOUR. It Takes a Citywide Church
1.b, 2.d, 3.d, 4.a, 5.c, 6.a, 7.d, 8.c.

CHAPTER FIVE

THREE SPIRITUAL ENEMIES OF UNITY

It is important to realize that, while we are dealing with the weakness of flesh and blood, our true fight is not against people, but "spiritual forces of wickedness" (Eph 6:12).

The issue is not the issue; the apparent enemy is not the real enemy. We are not fighting people, but the spirits that manipulate immature or sinful attitudes of heart in people. These spirits seek to gain access to our churches and families; they must be discerned. Religious ambition in the human heart is just the entry point for the enemies we are truly fighting: the spirits of division and strife.

The nature and goal of these spirits are the same: to inspire someone to seek in an ungodly way another person's position of authority, thus causing division. This is the ancient battle transported to modern times with flesh and blood role players. Recall Jude's warning,

> And angels who did not keep their own domain, but abandoned their proper abode, He has kept in eternal bonds under darkness for the judgment of the great day.   —Jude 1:6

When we unethically abandon our "proper abode" and seek the role of another, we are embracing the very sin Lucifer and his angels committed. Just as their sin led to hell, so their manipulation of earthly ambitions extends hell into the lives of men and women on earth.

While they share the same goal of creating division, their approaches to separating people are unique. The Old Testament provides three examples of individuals who usurped authority and divided the people of God: Korah, Absalom and Jezebel. Although these individuals were real people with historic lives, for the sake of classification we will assign their names to the spirits that manipulated them. When we discuss these enemies, we are looking through the human personality at the spirit which seeks to find modern counterparts, again bringing strife between God's people.

KORAH: THE LEADER WHO WANTS IT ALL

The New Testament writer Jude mentions specifically the "rebellion of Korah" (Jude 1:11). Korah was a leader in ancient Israel; he was equal to Aaron in authority and was a cousin to both Moses and Aaron. Through his influence, he was able to seduce 250 of Israel's princes to join him in a rebellion against Moses.

The worst divisions among God's people are those which are led by subordinate leaders who have acquired a large following. Matthew Henry's Commentary says of Korah and the other leaders in rebellion: "Note, the pride, ambition, and emulation, of great men have always been the occasion of a great deal of mischief both in churches and states . . . The fame and renown which they had did not content them; they were high, but would be higher, and thus the famous men became infamous."

Although Matthew Henry is speaking of Korah, clearly he could be describing Lucifer himself or any subordinate leader who has tasted of success, is discontent they do not have more power, and is envious of those above them. Beware when we desire the position of our leaders.

Listen to Korah's accusation against Moses and Aaron: "You take too much upon yourselves . . . Why then do you exalt yourselves above the assembly of the Lord?" (Num 16:3 NKJV) While it is Korah who is in rebellion, he charges that Moses is rebelling against God and is domineering in his leadership. It is Korah who is seeking to exalt himself, yet he accuses Moses and Aaron of exalting themselves "above the assembly."

As a means of spiritual discernment, listen carefully to the one who accuses your pastoral leadership. Even before you examine your pastor, examine his accuser. For you will often see in him the very flaws he says are in the pastor.

As a further argument, Korah states that "all the congregation is holy . . . and the Lord is among them" (Num 16:3 NKJV) The implication is that Korah is actually the one most concerned for the people, that Moses' task is complete, and it is time for new leadership to be appointed.

Of course, at this time all Israel was not holy nor was the assignment of Moses complete. But these things were said to reinforce the accusation that Moses was a domineering personality who was primarily seeking to maintain control of Israel.

Friends, there are times when a senior leader may truly be overly controlling, and we must not allow man to intimidate us. But there is another time when our wrong attitude toward authority will cause us to misjudge a leader as "controlling" when he is, in fact, simply fulfilling his God-given spiritual responsibility. God had appointed Moses as Israel's leader. God chose him on the basis of his meekness, a trait that was little esteemed by those who sought to remove him from leadership. Remember: to usurp the authority that God has installed is to sin against the Lord Himself.

Moses responded to Korah,

> Hear now, you sons of Levi, is it not enough for you that the God of Israel has separated you from the rest of the congregation of Israel, to bring you near to Himself, to do the service of the tabernacle of the Lord, and to stand before the congregation to minister to them; and that He has brought you near, Korah, and all your brothers, sons of Levi, with you? And are you seeking for the priesthood also?
> —Numbers 16:8–10

Moses exposes the sin of envy and ambition in Korah's heart. He asks, "Is it not enough for you" that you already have a position set apart to God? Ambition walks upon two legs: envy and pride. Whenever we covet the position God has assigned to another, we are attracting the Lord's anger to ourselves. Indeed, the story of Korah's rebellion concludes with the ground swallowing Korah and those in rebellion with him.

It is noteworthy that both Korah and Jethro, Moses' father-in-law, approached Moses with a similar statement. Korah was confrontational and filled with ambition and rebellion; Jethro was humble and filled with concern. When Jethro saw all that Moses was doing, he said, "What is this thing that you are doing for the people? Why do you alone sit as judge and all the people stand about you from morning until evening?" (Exod 18:14).

To express concern to a leader in a humble manner is an asset to any church; to confront the leader out of pride and ambition, as did Korah, is to expose yourself to the wrath of God. Under Jethro's counsel, Israel prospered. Never be afraid to submit your observations to leaders. Give your advice; then let them administrate it as they see fit.

An interesting side note was that the sons of Korah did not die in their father's rebellion. They chose, instead, to be submissive to Moses and Aaron. In time, the sons of Korah held a place of great honor in David's day, actually writing a number of the Psalms, which we study today as sacred Scriptures.

To be free from the influences of the Korah spirit, we must be content to wholeheartedly serve God where He has currently placed us. A time may come when a new order or new assignment comes to us from the Holy Spirit, but until then the Lord will not require us to challenge the authority of those over us nor divide the church so we can fulfill our religious ambitions.

The Absalom Spirit

Nelson's Bible Dictionary tells us that "Absalom was the third son by Maacah, the daughter of the king of Geshur (2 Sam 3:3; 1 Chron 3:2). Of royal descent on both sides, Absalom was a potential heir to the throne. Attractive in appearance and charming in manners, he was also a popular prince with the people and a favorite of his father."

However, although a favorite of his father and the people, Absalom suffered the injustice of his half sister's rape by Amnon, another of David's sons. In retaliation, Absalom had Amnon murdered by his servants. Fearing the wrath of his father for the murder of Amnon, he fled to Geshur, where he lived in exile for three years. Finally, under pressure from his leaders, David reluctantly sent for Absalom, yet shunned him when he returned. The long delay and his father's indifference produced a bitterness in Absalom toward the king, which ripened into a plan to steal his father's throne:

Absalom used to rise early and stand beside the way to the gate; and it happened that when any man had a suit to come to the king for judgment, Absalom would call to him and say, "From what city are you?" And he would say, "Your servant is from one of the tribes of Israel."

Then Absalom would say to him, "See, your claims are good and right, but no man listens to you on the part of the king." Moreover, Absalom would say, "Oh that one would appoint me judge in the land, then every man who has any suit or cause could come to me, and I would give him justice." And it happened that when a man came near to prostrate himself before him, he would put out his hand and take hold of him and kiss him. And in this manner Absalom dealt with all Israel who came to the king for judgment; so Absalom stole away the hearts of the men of Israel.

—2 Samuel 15:2–6

Just as Korah sought Moses' place, and Lucifer before him sought the place of God, so Prince Absalom sought the throne of King David. At first, however, Absalom was not openly confrontational of David, nor did he seek to challenge the king's authority. Rather, Absalom used his charm and subtle criticisms of the king to steal away the hearts of men.

Again, the New Testament writer Jude gives us an insight into this manipulating spirit as it manifests today through people:

These are grumblers, finding fault, following after their own lusts; they speak arrogantly, flattering people for the sake of gaining an advantage . . . These are the ones who cause divisions, worldly-minded, devoid of the Spirit.   —Jude 1:16, 19

Absalom found fault with David and engendered grumbling in the people of Israel, while winning the hearts of the people with flattery and charm. Jude said, "These are the ones who cause divisions." The plan of the Absalom spirit is simple: Grumble about the way things are not getting done, find fault with the leader, and arrogantly project the image that, if you were in charge, all would be well. Then, to capture the hearts of the people, flatter them and bring them into your camp. Paul also warned about those whom he called "wolves," who "will arise, speaking perverse things, to draw away the disciples after them" (Acts 20:29–30).

To speak "perverse things" means we have twisted or distorted the truth. Beware when someone comes along complaining about the way things are done, speaking evil of the church leader and promoting himself as an answer to these problems. You are probably listening to a wolf in the flock of God. Yet, even in this situation, speak with this person directly and expose his error. Perhaps the Lord will change his heart.

What if the suspicions raised against the senior leader seem to be true? Before you talk to anyone in the congregation, go to the leader himself according to Matthew 18. Go in meekness, entreating him "as a father" (1 Tim 5:1). Hear his side. If he is guilty of serious sin and remains unrepentant, bring with you two or three others. If he continues in sin, public exposure of his error is the final remedy (see Matt 18:15–17). But before you do that, your group should approach other church leaders in the city, or the denomination's district supervisor. Let them administrate the proper discipline.

At the same time, you must be certain he is in serious sin. It is not enough to just *sense* that there is *"something wrong under the surface."* You must have facts. If his primary "sin" is that he does not feel comfortable going along with the current trend in American Christianity, this is not sin. If you feel you must see certain spiritual manifestations in church, go somewhere where the things you seek are occurring, but do not divide your church, nor speak things to draw disciples after yourself. If you dream of being the leader of the church and are using spiritual phenomena to justify building a constituency, you are walking in the footsteps of Absalom, not Christ.

To free yourself from the influences of the Absalom spirit, repent of pride and refrain from using flattery to gain an advantage among the people. Instead of manipulating the unmet needs of the church to gain a following, submit yourself and your talents to the church leaders. Ask them how you can help. Don't exploit the needs; help meet them. And when you have been used by the Lord, point people to Christ, securing them in the care of the church leaders.

(For further insight on the nature of Absalom, read *A Tale of Three Kings* by Gene Edwards.)

THE JEZEBEL SPIRIT

In the Old Testament, Jezebel was a queen who fought against authority, whether that authority was resident in the spiritual leaders (the prophets) or the secular leader (the king). In the New Testament, Jesus mentions this spirit again, this time manifest as a prophetess in the church in Thyatira. In both settings, this spirit desires to neutralize authority and take control over other people in the church and family.

When the Jezebel spirit attacks church leadership, its ultimate purpose will be to disable the spiritual authority of pastoral leadership. The attack may come in the form of sexual temptation, confusion or prophetic manipulation, but its aim is to supplant the authority in the church.

Thus, Jesus promised that the church that overcomes Jezebel will be granted "authority over the nations" (Rev 2:26). The Jezebel spirit seeks to divide, diminish and then displace the spiritual authority God has given church leaders.

While Korah and Absalom use issues that most often affect men, Jezebel targets women. In the New Testament, Jesus Himself referred to Jezebel as a "woman . . . who calls herself a prophetess" (Rev 2:20). Catch this phrase, she "calls herself." In other words, she is self-appointed and submitted to no one. She uses her prophetic insights and sensitivities to draw a following to herself, again dividing the church from its true base of authority.

If you are a woman who has a propensity to gain control in relationships, the antidote for this influence is true humility. Let the Lord promote you. Stay submissive. Jezebel's quest for control masks a deeper need she has concerning fear. She was probably abused and is afraid of being abused again, so she seeks to control her world using whatever means available. To be healed from the influence of Jezebel, whether it attaches itself to a woman or a man, one must truly learn to trust God.

Because this spirit wars against authority in the church, it will seek to put wedges of division between a pastor and the church intercessors. To counter this potential division, let the senior leader appreciate, communicate and support his intercessors and esteem their contribution; and let the intercessors set their prayer focus to seek the spiritual fulfillment of their pastor's vision.

Without pastors leading in godly authority, a church simply cannot function: confusion, ambition and chaos reign. True spiritual authority is a source of protection; it is a living shelter that covers and nurtures a home or church. Satan seeks to neutralize the leader in that Christian setting, for if he can strike the shepherd, he can scatter the sheep.

And, we need intercessors, for prayer is the frontier of transformation; without intercessors, the church literally would not move forward. However, when an intercessor assumes that their "prophetic witness" is the guiding light of the church, or when they stand apart from the church leader and promote a different vision than what the leadership presents, it is a sign that the spirit of Jezebel may be trying to divide that church.

Indeed, the confusion spreads, as those who present a vision different from the pastor's are usually presenting something that seems godly and reasonable. Yet, the unbending demand that a leader conform to a prophetic witness, or the urgency of its timing, is where the enemy gains access and causes division. So, simply submit your witness to the church leaders and trust God to bring it to pass, if He so chooses, in its proper time.

Intercessors must accept that God has given the church leadership the responsibility to guide the church. The senior leader may draw his vision for the church directly from the Lord or indirectly from his staff. He may find direction from Christian authors, denominational leadership, or some combination of the above. Not the least of his resources, however, are the church intercessors. I personally have been rescued and protected by the faithfulness of humble intercessors who stand in the gap before God on my behalf.

Yet, when an intercessor quietly bypasses the church leadership and seeks to introduce a different vision than that which is currently guiding the church, they are introducing strife and confusion to God's people. As an intercessor myself, let me urge you to simply submit your perceptions and spiritual aspirations to the church leaders. If any change of direction is to come, it should come through their administration.

Intercessors, make your stand to defend the word spoken from the pulpit by the pastor. If his teaching is boring and unimaginative, all the more reason to pray. Take his or her sermon and focus your prayer on that theme during the coming week. There is nothing more powerful than when the teaching in a church and the intercession of that church are in agreement (see Zech 12:10; 1 Peter 4:11). Indeed, small wonder Jezebel seeks to divide the intercessors from the leaders. For when intercessors pray what the pastor preaches, the union of the Spirit and the Word release the creative power of heaven itself.

Let's pray: *Lord, help me to see and understand my role in Your kingdom. Master, grant me the meekness of the Holy Spirit, that I might serve without ambition, encourage without manipulation, and intercede without trying to control. Lord, help me to walk in discernment. Free me from any influence other than the ministry of the Holy Spirit Himself. In Jesus' name. Amen.*

—FROM THE BOOK, *IT'S TIME TO END CHURCH SPLITS*

SELF TEST, CHAPTER FIVE

Remember, we are looking for answers that correspond with this training. Please write out your essay answers, allowing the Holy Spirit to provoke your thoughts. You may want to use them for group discussion. Note: we do not provide answers to essay questions. To check your multiple choice answers, see answer key in the next session.

Chapter 5, Essay #1: Who should we examine before we examine our senior leader. Why?

Chapter 5, Essay #2: Make a quick list of some of the ungodly attributes of Korah, Absalom and Jezebel.

1. What gives entry for the spirits of division and strife to manipulate?
   a. religious ambition
   b. immature sinful attitudes of heart
   c. contentment in where He has us
   d. both a & b

2. When we unethically abandon our "prayer abode" and seek the role of another, we are embracing:
    a. the very sin Lucifer and his angels committed
    b. change and growth
    c. an attitude of Christlikeness
    d. the beginning of the citywide church

3. Who are three individuals the O.T. provides as examples of ones who usurped authority, creating division?
    a. Maacah, Ahab, Geshur
    b. Jethro, Amnon, Geshur
    c. Korah, Absalom, Jezebel
    d. Moses, Jehu, Reuben

4. While these manipulating spirits share the same goal of creating division, their _____ are unique.
    a. ambitions
    b. approaches to separate people
    c. aspirations
    d. all the above

5. What are some characteristics or "approaches to separate" that are unique to Korah?
    a. was a subordinate leader who acquired a large following
    b. confrontational of authority, with accusations
    c. conformity to leader's vision
    d. both a & b

6. If you listen carefully, examining the one who is accusing another, you will often see in the accuser:
    a. the very flaws he accuses his leader of
    b. meekness
    c. purity of motivation
    d. humility

7. To usurp the authority God has installed is:
    a. envy, ambition and pride
    b. to sin against the Lord Himself
    c. advancing God's kingdom
    d. both a & b

8. To be free from the influences of the Korah spirit, we must:
    a. fight for our rights
    b. be content to wholeheartedly serve God where He has currently placed us
    c. look for a new position in ministry
    d. both a & c

9. What are some characteristics or "approaches to separate" that are unique to Absalom?
   a. was never popular or appealing in mannerisms
   b. potential leader (heir to throne)
   c. used flattery, charm and subtle criticisms to win hearts
   d. both b & c

10. What are some characteristics or "approaches to separate" that are unique to Jezebel?
   a. self-appointed, submitted to no one
   b. attacks in the form of sexual temptation, confusion, or prophetic manipulation
   c. assumes their prophetic witness is the guiding light and has unbending demand that a leader conform to a prophetic witness
   d. all the above

> QUOTE:
>
> *"There is nothing more powerful than when the teaching in a church and the intercession of that church are in agreement."*

SESSION FOUR:

UNDERSTANDING AUTHORITY

SESSION FOUR AUDIO MESSAGES:

4a. The Freedom of Authority
4b. The Perfection of Submission

ANSWER KEY TO LAST SESSION'S
SELF TEST QUESTIONS:

CHAPTER FIVE. Three Spiritual Enemies of Unity
1.d, 2.a, 3.c, 4.b, 5.d, 6.a, 7.d, 8.b, 9.d, 10.d.

CHAPTER SIX

A GOD OF ORDER

"For this reason I left you in Crete, that you might set in order what remains" (Titus 1:5).

I want to talk about a prominent aspect of the Father's nature and our corresponding need to understand the realm of authority. For some, the mere mention of the word *authority* awakens fear, so before we begin, let me ask you for grace. If possible, please consider what I present without forming your opinion until I'm done.

THE VALUE OF FREEDOM

Before we discuss authority, I want to counterbalance my words with another truth concerning our spiritual freedom in Christ. First, when the Spirit of God begins His transforming work, He starts with individuals. We are not faceless numbers to the Father, but beloved children. Indeed, Jesus assures us that His sheep know His voice as He calls them each by name (see John 10:26–28).

As unique souls, we are important to the Lord. He hears our individual cries when we pray; He knows our unique needs when we struggle. As individuals, we are valued by God. The Father's original purpose was to make us in His image; at the core of the divine nature is true, spiritual freedom. As Paul wrote, "It was for freedom that Christ set us free" (Gal 5:1).

We will misunderstand what this chapter is about unless we read it as spiritually free people. God does not want us to "look" outwardly righteous, yet inwardly be in bondage. He wants us free, in bondage to no one or any thing but God Himself. You see, if our righteousness is only because the pastor or other Christians are looking, we are shallow indeed. Jesus came to set captives free and bring liberty to prisoners. God wants us to be individuals who, in the power of the Holy Spirit, have control over our mind, will and emotions. He especially does not want us subservient to the intimidations or manipulations of man.

The Father sets us perfectly free so, in true freedom, we can choose conformity to the Son of God. Christlikeness is our choice, our liberty, and our destiny.

Therefore, when we discuss order, authority and submission issues, I pray that you hear my words as free people who have a clear vision of becoming Christlike. As such, you have the right to go to any church or no church at all; you are free to throw this book against a wall or read only what you want. No one can exclude you from their church because, from the moment you were born again, God enrolled you in the "church of the first-born," which is in heaven (see Heb 12:22–23).

But, it is one thing to be assured of salvation; it is another to attain the likeness of Christ. If we will, in truth, become Christlike, we must see with revelation the reasons why our Father calls us to honor the order in our local church and why the way to exercising Christlike authority is bowing in Christlike submission.

Having secured ourselves in the freedom given us in Christ, let us turn our eyes upon the Father. One cannot truly know God nor appreciate Him as He is without being awed at the ordered array of His universe. The life we enjoy in its splendor and variety is built upon a substructure of immutable order. The God who created animals, vegetation and people also created the subatomic worlds and the unchanging laws of physics.

When something is "ordered," it's because someone is in authority. We may imagine ourselves in the afterlife enjoying the great pleasures of heaven, but there is authority in heaven. Heaven itself is ordered with an angelic hierarchy that includes archangels, seraphim, cherubim, thrones, dominions, principalities, powers, virtues and angels. Each of these spirit-beings represents a level of authority in God's kingdom. Remember, heaven is not like earth. Most of earth's population follows their own will as they decide life's choices; in heaven, only one will is done: God's. If you don't like this idea, you can't go to heaven, for only those who do God's will are going to enter the kingdom of God (see Matt 7:21).

Of course, doing God's will unites the reason we were created with the joy of serving the Creator. God matches our gifts and skills with opportunities to fulfill them; and while we accomplish the tasks we were created to fulfill, we cannot help but worship Him. But still, only one will is done.

I am saying this because this same God of order, who created the ordered universe and the hierarchy of angels in heaven, also conceived and designed the church. In fact, originally "church" was an extension of God's ordered domain: the kingdom of heaven on earth. Thus, when we read the book of Acts, we see that the people in the early church were part of this ordered domain:

united "with one mind" and "with one accord" (Acts 1:14; 4:24, 32; 5:12). Because heaven is ordered, and the Lord is a God of order, the church was an ordered society where authority and submission were simply accepted on earth as it is in heaven.

One may argue, "If we had their power, we'd be united as well." Let me emphasize, they were of one mind *before* Pentecost (see Acts 1:14). If there had not been unity among the disciples prior to Pentecost, there would not have been an outpouring of the Holy Spirit on Pentecost. The outpouring did not create unity; unity made the way for the outpouring. The order was first, then came the power of the Spirit.

This principle of having order before power can also be seen by studying the Israelites who conquered Canaan, and also David, who with his mighty men united Israel and extended her boundaries. In both cases, unity preceded power. Central to the empowering of people to attain their destiny was their ability to submit to the leaders God had appointed. There simply cannot be sustainable unity without authority and submission.

Let me take this a little further. While the Lord sits in the heavens and does whatever He pleases, yet repeatedly the Scriptures confirm that it pleases the Lord to honor the order He creates and work within its protocols. Consider: the Lord appeared to Paul, spoke to him, actually blinded him in His glory, and then said, "Rise, and enter the city, and it shall be told you what you must do" (Acts 9:6).

Why didn't the Lord just tell Paul what he had to do? Paul would have to learn about God, at least initially, as he submitted to other Christian leaders. This is God's order and the Lord Himself honored it. Paul had to hear about Jesus from Ananias, a man who was a Christian before him.

Or consider Cornelius: an angel appeared to this Roman centurion in a dream and told him that a man named Simon Peter would explain to him the way of salvation. Why didn't the angel simply tell Cornelius about Jesus? Cornelius would be the first European convert, but God had begun the church with the Jews. Before the Gentiles could enter the kingdom en masse they would hear of Christ from the Jews, who first accepted the Messiah. God honored the order He created, which was to present the gospel "to the Jew first and also to the Greek" (Rom 1:16; 2:10).

Consider church protocol in the book of Acts. When Philip brought the gospel to Samaria, miracles, conversions and great signs were accomplished. But Philip would not lay his hands upon the Samaritans to receive the Holy Spirit. Why? Because until this time, the Holy Spirit had only spread through the hands of the first apostles. Again, God required His servant to respect the order and authority of the first apostles.

Or consider the order in Jesus' family. The angel Gabriel spoke to Mary, revealing that, through the Holy Spirit, she would conceive the Son of God. Yet, from the time Mary married Joseph, God spoke only to him concerning direction for the family. Angels assured him Mary's pregnancy was from God; he received dreams and angelic warnings telling him to leave Israel and warnings that instructed him when to return.

God honored the order of the family—because Adam was created first, then Eve. Yes, the Lord still works when conditions are out of order, because He honors faith. But just because He accommodates our weaknesses, we should not assume He will endorse them with the fullness of His power.

Consider the life of Christ Himself. As a child, He grew up "in subjection" to His parents (see

Luke 2:51). He also was submissive to the instructions of the rabbis and, as was His custom, He faithfully participated in the Sabbath readings at the synagogue (see Luke 4:16). Jesus simply was not a rebel. At the Jordan River, He submitted Himself to the ministry of John the Baptist, though He was John's spiritual superior. Yet, to "fulfill all righteousness," He eagerly submitted Himself. *Indeed, it was while He humbled Himself to a lesser ministry that the flood of the Father's pleasure, together with the Holy Spirit, descended upon Him* (see Matt 3:13–17).

I know what I am about to say will seem over the line to many, but Jesus did not instruct His followers to rebel even against false religious authority. Listen to what He taught, "The scribes and the Pharisees have seated themselves in the chair of Moses." On their own, the Pharisees assumed an authority that God had not given them. Yet listen to how Jesus tells His disciples to relate to false authority: "Therefore all that they tell you, do and observe, but do not do according to their deeds; for they say things, and do not do them" (Matt 23:3).

Amazingly, Jesus instructed both His disciples and the larger multitude to "do and observe" all that the Pharisees taught. I don't believe in any way He intended for His disciples to remain with the Pharisees, but the implication in Jesus' statement is this: as long as you are Jewish and attending temple services, the Pharisees are in charge and here's how to relate. Submit to them, but do not become like them.

Even though their authority was questionable and their behavior hypocritical, He did not say to disrespect them, but rather to not do as they do. Yes, Jesus Himself confronted the Pharisees harshly. However, Jesus was not raising up a people to be known for their confrontational attitudes;

they were to be known for their strength of character and their love.

Again, when Jesus stood before Pilate, He showed Himself meek, like a lamb. Pilate challenged Him, " 'Do You not know that I have authority to release You, and I have authority to crucify You?' Jesus answered, 'You would have no authority over Me, unless it had been given you from above' " (John 19:10–11).

Jesus knew that all authority in the universe—the very realm of authority—was under the domain of the Father's watchful gaze (see Rom 13:1). While authority itself could be misused, still the Father's authority transcended human authority and could, with great power, override the imperfections of man. Thus, Jesus was not afraid to submit to people who were spiritually less than Himself because He knew God's greater authority would transform injustice to justice.

In the Godhead, the Father exists as God in authority; the Son exists as God in submission. Jesus, you recall, only did the things He saw the Father do; everything about Christ was an act of obedience and submission. Christ reveals how God submits to God. In this submission is peace; Jesus rested in the Father's watchful gaze. The issues were never between Jesus and other men, but between Himself and the Father.

When Jesus suffered the injustice of His trial, He didn't blame Pilate, the Pharisees, His disciples or the multitudes. He didn't even blame the devil. Instead, Peter tells us that while Jesus was "being reviled, He did not revile in return; while suffering, He uttered no threats, but kept entrusting Himself to Him who judges righteously" (1 Pet 2:23).

Peter uses Christ's example of submission to tell the church,

Keep your behavior excellent among the Gentiles . . . Submit yourselves for the Lord's sake to every human institution, whether to a king as the one in authority, or to governors as sent by him for the punishment of evildoers and the praise of those who do right.   —1 Peter 2:12–14

He continues,

Act as free men, and do not use your freedom as a covering for evil, but use it as bondslaves of God. Honor all men; love the brotherhood, fear God, honor the king. Servants, be submissive to your masters with all respect, not only to those who are good and gentle, but also to those who are unreasonable.   —1 Peter 2:16–18

Did Christ's faith work? Of course! In the first century the cross was the symbol of torture, death and utter hopelessness. Because Jesus trusted the Father's authority to override the misuse of authority, the cross today is the symbol of redemption, resurrection and hope.

Beloved, the Lord is a God of order and, for His purposes, He requires we submit to authority and order, whether it's in the secular world, the family or the church. Listen carefully: rebellion is not a virtue. Submission was clearly the pattern in Jesus' life. He revealed how God would submit to God and, in so doing, set the pattern for us, who are created in His image.

Let's pray: *Lord, forgive me for my insolence toward those in authority. I confess that I have not trusted nor understood the realm of authority, but I ask that You forgive me. Help me to ever keep my eyes upon You, trusting Your ability to take my submitted, believing heart through every injustice and into the realm of redemption and power. In Jesus' name. Amen.*

—FROM THE BOOK, *IT'S TIME TO END CHURCH SPLITS*

SELF TEST, CHAPTER SIX

Remember, we are looking for answers that correspond with this training. Please write out your essay answers, allowing the Holy Spirit to provoke your thoughts. You may want to use them for group discussion. Note: we do not provide answers to essay questions. To check your multiple choice answers, see answer key in the next session.

Chapter 6, Essay #1: Briefly describe Christ's submissiveness from his childhood until the time the Holy Spirit descended upon Him.

Chapter 6, Essay #2: Cite two biblical examples where order preceded power.

1. The way to exercising Christlike authority is:
    a. coercive leadership
    b. bowing in Christlike submission
    c. being unyielding in vision
    d. both b & c

2. How is the authority and ordered hierarchy in heaven unlike life on earth?
    a. most of earth's population follows their own will as they decide life's choices
    b. in heaven, the principalities rule
    c. in heaven, only God's will is done
    d. both a & c

3. What is an example of an extension of God's ordered domain, "the kingdom of heaven on earth"?
    a. a church where no one is allowed to laugh
    b. the early church in Acts, united "with one mind" and "with one accord"
    c. a church where love, authority and submission are accepted as it is in heaven
    d. both b & c

4. What principle precedes power?
    a. order, ability to submit to the leaders God has appointed
    b. unity, being of one mind
    c. separation of denominations
    d. both a & b

5. When was it that the flood of the Father's pleasure, together with the Holy Spirit, descended upon Jesus?
    a. while confronting the Pharisees
    b. when He stood before Pilate
    c. while He humbled Himself, submitting to a lesser ministry
    d. when Paul heard of Jesus through Ananias

6. Why was Jesus not afraid to submit to people who were spiritually less than Himself?
   a. He trusted God's greater authority, seeing the Father's authority presiding over all things in His life
   b. He was fearless and did not care what they did to Him
   c. He wanted to use submission to bring justice
   d. He wanted God to judge those who misused authority

7. What does Peter tell the church about being submissive to our masters?
   a. be submissive selectively to those who praise us
   b. be submissive with respect and only to those who are good, gentle and reasonable
   c. be submissive with all respect, not only to those who are good and gentle, but also to those who are unreasonable
   d. be submissive and become like them, whether to a king or governors

8. How did Jesus instruct the disciples and the larger multitude to act toward the Pharisees' being in charge?
   a. disrespect them
   b. submit to them, but do not become like them
   c. disregard all that the Pharisees taught
   d. do not even observe false religious authority

QUOTE:

"The Lord is a God of order and, for His purposes, He requires we submit to authority and order, whether it's in the secular world, the family or the church."

CHAPTER SEVEN

CHRISTLIKE SUBMISSION

Our submission to authority is not born of fear nor intimidation. True submission comes from revelation and an understanding of the character of Jesus Christ. It is a means of rapid growth and imparted grace.

Jesus had full possession of His soul; He didn't react to man; He fully trusted God. Thus, He could submit to man's frail systems and miscarriages of authority, knowing the Father would ultimately judge righteously and transform the injustice. Where Lucifer demanded full independence from the authority of God, Jesus was perfectly yielded to the Father's authority (see 2 Cor 13:4).

Now, I know that some are afraid to embrace a submissive attitude of heart. They worry that they'll have to blindly submit to the antichrist or be forced, cult-like, into all manner of sin, including sexual. We have only to consider the recent sex scandals in the Catholic Church and the misuse of authority among the priests to shudder with legitimate concern.

So, let me reinforce this truth: Jesus never submitted to authority that would cause Him to sin, nor did He expect His disciples to sin if one in authority ordered them. Just as you *choose* to submit, so you *choose* to not submit to one telling you to sin. If your employer asks you to lie for him, you can maintain a submissive attitude while telling him, "No, I can't do that." Yet, even here our motive is not to rebel against man, but to submit on a higher level to God.

Another fear is that, by submitting to another person, we will lose ourselves and become like them. In fact, when we submit to the anointing upon a person, we gain more than we invest. Elisha received a double portion of Elijah's anointing because he passionately and faithfully submitted himself to his mentor's anointing. Bear in mind, Elijah was the opposite personality type of Elisha. Yet, by submitting, he doubled the accomplishments of Elijah.

You see, what we possess of spiritual power is already ours, but it is limited. By putting ourselves in submission to another, we gain some measure of the other person's anointing. Elisha did not lose his own identity by submitting; he did not become a "little Elijah." He still retained his own personality and approach to ministry except, when his ministry began, he had twice as much power.

We fear that by being submissive, we will be asked to give more than we receive. Again, the opposite is true. Jesus taught, "He who receives a prophet in the name of a prophet shall receive a prophet's reward" (Matt 10:41). Submission is the vehicle for receiving. God rewards a prophet, not only in the world to come, but also here. The "prophet's reward" represents the unique power dimension a man or woman of God has purchased with sacrifice and suffering. Just by submitting ourselves, by humbly "receiving" from them, we can obtain without cost a measure of the prophet's reward.

Remember: the multitudes did not know Jesus was the Son of God; they didn't understand "by His stripes" they would be healed (Isa 53:5 NKJV).

They did just one thing: they submitted to Christ for healing and received the "prophet's reward." The Pharisees, on the other hand, did not receive Christ; thus, their unsubmitted attitude disqualified them from receiving the benefits of Jesus' power.

When a church submits to me, I assume an added responsibility. It does not mean that I, as a leader, control their now mindless lives. How opposite the truth is! A person submitted to my authority is one for whom I pray more frequently; when they are sick, I visit them. When they weep, I cry with them; and where they are immature, I give myself to training them, instructing them in the mysteries of life. The submitted person is the beneficiary of the relationship, much more than the one in authority.

We have seen the abuses of authority, and it has made many of us wary and resistant to the true benefits of submission and impartation. But let's take this a step further. You do not need to actually have a man or woman of God in front of you to be submitted to their anointing. When I was a young man and new in Christ, I would take books by Andrew Murray or Watchman Nee, then kneel at the foot of my bed and read their words. I often felt that I was drinking in, through the Holy Spirit, the substance of their anointing. You see, I didn't just read their words, I submitted myself to their teaching.

So, consider submission to be the free choice of a wise person who sees something Christlike in another's life and has asked to receive it. Submission does not diminish us; it doubles us. It extends the boundaries of our spirituality into the lives of people whom we see were transformed by Christ—and allows what they have received from Him to be imparted to us as well.

Let's pray: *Lord, what a storehouse of riches Your church is! To think that when You ascended on high, You gave gifts to men, spiritual leaders, who could advance my spiritual growth simply by my submission. Master, let my eyes be ever on You and let me follow men only as they follow You. Amen.*

—FROM THE BOOK, *IT'S TIME TO END CHURCH SPLITS*

SELF TEST, CHAPTER SEVEN

Remember, we are looking for answers that correspond with this training. Please write out your essay answers, allowing the Holy Spirit to provoke your thoughts. You may want to use them for group discussion. Note: we do not provide answers to essay questions. To check your multiple choice answers, see answer key in the next session.

Chapter 7, Essay #1: Reflect on your understanding of submission before and after studying this chapter.

Chapter 7, Essay #2: What are the blessings the Lord provides to those who remain submissive?

1. True submission to authority is born out of:
     a. fear and intimidation
     b. revelation and an understanding of the character of Jesus Christ
     c. full independence from the authority of God
     d. unyielding faith in our own abilities to minister to others

2. What are some fears that hinder us from embracing submission and the growth received through it?
     a. concern we will have to blindly submit
     b. fear we will be asked to give more than we receive
     c. fear we will lose who we are and become like other people
     d. all the above

3. When is it acceptable to choose not to submit?
     a. when an authority is teaching false doctrines
     b. when authority tells us to sin
     c. when a leader corrects us
     d. both a & b

4. What do we gain by putting ourselves in submission to another?
     a. disappearance of our own identity
     b. their respect
     c. some measure of the other person's anointing
     d. we don't gain anything; they do

5. What should we consider submission to be?
   a. the free choice of a wise person who sees something Christlike in another's life and has asked to receive it
   b. an act that diminishes us
   c. opportunity for advancement of our spiritual growth
   d. both a & c

6. When a person is submitted to their pastor, they become:
   a. subdued
   b. the beneficiary of the relationship
   c. one for whom the pastor assumes added responsibility; he prays for, weeps with, and gives himself to training
   d. both b & c

7. According to Pastor Francis' example when he was new in Christ, how can we also be submitted to a leader's anointing even if they aren't actually in front of us?
   a. praying they will come to our church
   b. keeping our distance
   c. submitting ourselves to their teaching, through the Holy Spirit drinking in the substance of their anointing from books, etc.
   d. remaining in the back of the church

8. What is the "prophet's reward" in Matthew 10:41 referring to?
   a. the unique power dimension a man or woman of God has purchased with sacrifice and suffering, which others can receive a measure of by submission
   b. the reward a pastor gives those who bring excellent prophetic words
   c. being rejected in their hometown
   d. the reward we receive only when we get to heaven

QUOTE:

"Elisha did not lose his own identity by submitting; he did not become a 'little Elijah.' He still retained his own personality and approach to ministry except, when his ministry began, he had twice as much power."

Session Five:

The Enemy's Subtleties

SESSION FIVE AUDIO MESSAGES:

5a. Breaking the Spirit of Strife
5b. More of God (part 2)

ANSWER KEY TO LAST SESSION'S
SELF TEST QUESTIONS:

CHAPTER SIX. A God of Order
1.b, 2.d, 3.d, 4.d, 5.c, 6.a, 7.c, 8.b.
CHAPTER SEVEN. Christlike Submission
1.b, 2.d, 3.d, 4.c, 5.d, 6.d, 7.c, 8.a.

CHAPTER EIGHT

THE DECEPTION SURROUNDING DIVISION

The Bible has a great deal to say about unity. However, I have yet to find one New Testament example where the Scriptures encourage born-again Christians to divide from each other. The Lord *multiplied* the church and *added* to their numbers; He did not divide His people.

LET THE WORD BE TRUE

For over thirty years I have witnessed many Scriptures taken out of context and twisted to suit the purpose of division. Yet, if we simply read objectively, we will not find one place where the Spirit of God inspired a faction within a church to divide and start another group, even if the first group was imperfect.

Dividing a church has no scriptural precedent. Just as people are deceived in their motives when they divide Christ's church, so they are deceived when they read the Scriptures seeking to justify themselves.

For instance, I have frequently heard quoted Paul's admonition, "Come out from their midst and be separate" (2 Cor 6:17). However, the apostle was not speaking of being separated from other

Christians. Rather, his purpose was to warn Christians about being "unequally yoked" with pagans or "unbelievers" (see 2 Cor 6:14–15 KJV).

Interestingly, the Old Testament version of this same verse was used by the Pharisees to justify their condescending attitude toward other Jews. In fact, the name *Pharisee* literally translated means "the separate." Jesus warned of those who "trusted in themselves that they were righteous, and viewed others with contempt" (Luke 18:9). This attitude of self-righteous contempt is often what motivates a faction to think of itself as more spiritual than another, and thus justify being "separate."

Another historic misinterpretation comes from First Corinthians, chapter 11, as Paul seems to concede that divisions and splits were almost necessary. He wrote: "I hear that divisions exist among you; and in part, I believe it. For there must also be factions among you, in order that those who are approved may have become evident among you" (1 Cor 11:18b–19).

Certainly, isolated by itself, the idea that there "must also be factions . . . that those who are approved may have become evident" adds legitimacy to the idea of divisions and splits. Of course, those who split from others always identify themselves as "those who are approved."

However, the actual context of the verse reveals the apostle's true perception and view. Here's the complete eighteenth verse: "For, in the first place, when you come together as a church, I hear that divisions exist among you; and in part, I believe it" (1 Cor 11:18).

Listen carefully to Paul's backdrop of unity upon which he isolates the problem of divisions. He introduces his thoughts by saying, "When you come together as a church . . ." Don't rush past his opening address. They hadn't split from each other; they were not meeting in different buildings, each with a unique name on a corner sign. They were still united and they all still would "come together as a church." In fact, until the split between Constantinople and Rome two hundred years later, there was only the one Christian church.

Paul wasn't justifying the divisions among them. In fact, the primary theme of First Corinthians is to reestablish unity (see chapters 1, 3, 8, 10:16–24, 11, 12, 13, 14). He wrote specifically to *correct* their divisions. But even though, in their carnality, some were followers of Paul while others followed Apollos or Cephas, they still came "together as a church." Paul's goal in this letter was to get them to see past the leaders who brought them into the kingdom and look at the King!

Every week the Christians in Corinth met together for worship, a love feast and weekly communion. It was here, in the administration of food, that they had broken into the cliques and factions that Paul identified as "approved." Some, indeed, tried to keep their focus on the significance of the Lord's Supper, while others were devouring as much as they could during the community meal (see 1 Cor 11:20–22, 33–34)!

In no way had Paul suddenly altered his course and decided that divisions were not a bad thing after all. Rather, he was acknowledging that the more gluttonous Christians had become a separate group within the church. In contrast, the Christians who reverently waited unintentionally became a group as well. This was not by premeditated design or organizational intent, but by their self-discipline and composure. Just as cream rises to the top of milk, so within the church there were those whose spirituality gave contrast to the carnality of others—and those were the ones who were approved. But they didn't divide from the others and form a new church within the church. Paul didn't urge them to separate from the others, for they all still "came together as a church."

Indeed, in the very next chapter, Paul reiterates his theme of unity, using the analogy of a body that is diverse, yet interdependently united. Everything he has written to this point is captured in his summary-thought in verse 25. Listen again to his heart:

> That there should be no schism in the body; but that the members should have the same care one for another.
> —1 Corinthians 12:25 KJV

Beloved, the word translated "schism" in the King James (rendered "division" in the NAS), means "split" in the Greek language. Translated literally, Paul is saying "there should be no split in the body."

What part of "no" don't we understand? Unity is the central theme of First Corinthians. How could one honestly ignore entire chapters about unity and take one half-verse out of context to justify a split? (see 1 Cor 11:18b) This is willful deception.

The Goal is Unity

In all that the New Testament declares for Christians—in all of the epistles and pastoral letters of Paul and the other apostles—the call is clearly, unmistakably toward unity, not division. There is a hurricane of spiritual truth blowing, bending and pushing the church in the direction of oneness with each other in Christ. The repeated rebuke throughout the Scriptures comes because of disunity and sectarianism.

Another verse used to justify splitting a church comes from Jesus Himself. He said, "Do you suppose that I came to grant peace on earth? I tell you, no, but rather division" (Luke 12:51). Jesus is not talking about dividing His people, but dividing those who follow Him from those who do not. Jesus does indeed separate us from the world, however He eternally unites us to Himself and one another.

As I searched through the New Testament on the subject of Christian unity, there were literally hundreds of verses pointing toward oneness in the born-again church. After years of study on this subject, I have yet to read one verse that instructed a group of Christians to slander, divide and split from another group of Christians in a city. If a pastor was practicing blatant sin, such as adultery or some crime which leads to imprisonment, then the other church leaders should remove that man. If he refuses to step down, then the church should regroup under new leadership, but these are extreme situations.

If God's Word calls us to unity with other born-again Christians throughout an entire city, how much more does this same command apply to relationships in a local church?

Yet, we need to realize that we are all different, with differing strengths and passions. Part of unity means we can accept that some people within our church community may desire to function differently than others. This diversity need not become disunity. We must defend the right to be unique, with differing tasks. Yet, diversity must find its expression without contention or strife.

The test for leaders and congregations is to find creative ways to facilitate diversity while remaining united. If unity of purpose cannot be maintained within a body of people, a church plant born of love and done with wisdom in the Lord's timing is a creative possibility.

ONE EXAMPLE

Several years ago I approached one of our associate pastors at River of Life, Marty Boller, and asked if he was praying about moving out of state. He said, "Yes." Marty had been a Vineyard pastor who merged his congregation with us and now, seven years later, he wanted to return to the Vineyard association of churches. Yet Marty did not want to sow division in our community, so he planned on moving to Canada to start his church!

Because he was an honorable man and very committed to unity, I suggested he take a few months and explain his vision in a weekly class with those from our church who were interested. When Marty started a new work in our city, he did so with a dozen or so River of Life families, and others. Today, we remain great friends and serve together in many citywide projects. We are closer because he was patient, wise and non-divisive.

There are many creative ways to multiply a church as long as we stay Christlike. It's when pride or ambition enter that division soon follows.

A PURER FIRST CENTURY CHURCH?

The argument arises that the church was much purer in its early years than it is now—so today we need to separate from others because of sin in the camp. The church in Jerusalem, in its inception, certainly set a standard for us all. However, as the church expanded to other cities and cultures, there were many problems; in some cases, their failures were worse than our own. Yet, the apostles who served Christ's church still called for unity in spite of the churches' imperfections.

Even in Jesus' address to the seven churches in the Revelation of John, though sin existed in the churches in five cities, Christ never instructed the innocent to break from the sinners. Rather, He commended those who walked in purity and left them in the midst of the sinful as an example of His righteousness.

Another argument used to justify splits has to do with doctrinal interpretation. Let me make it clear that our doctrines are very important—they define our belief systems and open the door to spiritual realities and levels of blessedness of which we would be otherwise ignorant. Having clear biblically based doctrines also provide boundaries to keep us from deception and half truths.

However, there are both core truths and peripheral truths to our faith. There are precepts that we must be willing to die for, yet there are other instructions that good Christians interpret differently. Because we are all learning, we must be willing to yield and stay humble.

In practical terms, we cannot be united with those who do not believe in the deity of Christ. Yet, we certainly can maintain the unity of the Spirit, for instance, with someone who has a different view about the timing of the Rapture. We cannot dilute God's truth concerning the new covenant, the inspiration of the Scriptures, the centrality of Jesus Christ, the atonement of His cross, His bodily resurrection, His physical return, salvation by grace through faith, the Trinity and the indwelling work of the Holy Spirit. But we are still learning about spiritual gifts, effective church government, signs and wonders, styles of praise, and various programs that train youth and make disciples of adults.

When Jesus defined the requirements for unity in John 17, He said our oneness would arise from three core realities. He said spiritual oneness would come as we believed in His name, His Word and His glory (see John 17:11, 20–22). These fundamental truths, if adhered to, He said, would unite His people.

However, to split a church because of a disagreement concerning peripheral doctrines is a smoke screen. It is a deception. There are those who argue they are taking their stand in defense of God's Word. Yet, how can they divide a church in defiance of God's Word? A person who will split a church over a nonfundamental doctrine or over a spiritual gift or style of worship is deceived and seeking to deceive others.

Let's pray: *Lord, forgive us for accepting divisions. Heal Your church, O God! Bring us into Christ-centered unity, that the world would believe in Your power. Amen.*

—FROM THE BOOK, *It's Time to End Church Splits*

SELF TEST, CHAPTER EIGHT

Remember, we are looking for answers that correspond with this training. Please write out your essay answers, allowing the Holy Spirit to provoke your thoughts. You may want to use them for group discussion. Note: we do not provide answers to essay questions. To check your multiple choice answers, see answer key in the next session.

Chapter 8, Essay #1: Give two frequent misinterpretations from First and Second Corinthians often used to try and justify church splits.

Chapter 8, Essay #2: Give a brief description of unity.

1. Jesus warned (in Luke 18:9) of what attitude that factions were motivated by and trusted as justification for being "separate"?
   a. modesty about their own spiritual maturity
   b. self-righteous contempt, to think of themselves as more spiritual than others
   c. esteeming others as better than ourselves
   d. desiring to be unequally yoked with pagans or unbelievers

2. What is the primary theme of First Corinthians?
   a. developing self-sufficiency of factions
   b. self-governed denominations
   c. reestablishing unity
   d. altering our focus toward our leader

3. What was Paul's goal in his letter to the Corinthians?
   a. to get them to see past the leaders who brought them into the kingdom and look at the King
   b. to help them know who was approved and not approved
   c. to help people find their niche
   d. to impart independence

4. Part of unity means we can accept _____.
   a. diversity
   b. contention and strife
   c. some people within the church will desire to function differently than others
   d. both a & c

5. Diversity must find its expression _____.
   a. forcibly
   b. without contention or strife
   c. in the worship
   d. apart from leadership

6. If unity of purpose cannot be maintained within a body of people, what is one creative possibility?
   a. start more small groups
   b. have two unique styles of services
   c. a church plant borne of love and done with wisdom in the Lord's timing
   d. provide a suggestion box

7. What are the three core realities Jesus defined in John 17 as requirements for unity?
   a. believing in His name, His Word and His glory
   b. agreeing on views of spiritual gifts, signs and wonders, pre-tribulation Rapture
   c. salvation by baptism, communion with unleavened bread, hymns
   d. an elder church government, altar calls, immersion baptism

QUOTE:

"There is a hurricane of spiritual truth blowing, bending and pushing the church in the direction of oneness with each other in Christ. The repeated rebuke throughout the Scriptures comes because of disunity and sectarianism."

CHAPTER NINE

ONE OF YOU IS A GOSSIP

"A perverse man spreads strife, and a slanderer separates intimate friends" (Prov 16:28).

Jesus made a remarkable statement concerning Judas when He said, " 'Did I Myself not choose you, the twelve, and yet one of you is a devil?' Now He meant Judas the son of Simon Iscariot, for he, one of the twelve, was going to betray Him" (John 6:70–71).

To what was Jesus referring when He identified Judas Iscariot as "a devil"? Was He speaking figuratively or factually? Is Jesus saying that a human being could not only "have" an evil spirit living in his soul, but that a person can actually become a demon?

Some teach that Judas had become so perfectly possessed by Satan that he actually lost his humanity. Before we accept this interpretation, let us remember that, after this fallen apostle delivered Jesus up, he felt such remorse for betraying Christ that he committed suicide. Could a demon feel such remorse for sin? I do not think so.

What I believe Jesus is identifying in Judas Iscariot as a "devil" is something that, today, exists unchecked among many Christians: *slander.* In the New Testament, the Greek word, *diabolos,* which is translated "devil" in this text, is translated impersonally elsewhere as a "false accuser," "slanderer" or "a malicious gossip." In fact, 1 Timothy 3:11 and 2 Timothy 3:3 both translate *diabolos* (Strong's #1228) as "malicious gossip(s)."

In other words, in my opinion, Jesus is not saying "one of you is a devil" in an organic or theological sense, but that one of you is "a slanderer, a malicious gossip." So, while the disciples were almost bragging about their loyalty to Christ, Jesus corrected them, in effect saying, "Yes, I chose you, but even among you there is one who is a malicious gossip, whose words will eventually betray Me to My enemies."

In the Last Days

This problem of gossip in the church, Paul tells us, will continue right into the end of the age. Listen carefully to what Paul wrote to Timothy about the last days: "Men will be lovers of self, lovers of money, boastful, arrogant, revilers, disobedient to parents, ungrateful, unholy, unloving, irreconcilable, malicious gossips" (2 Tim 3:2–3). In the midst of this list of great sins of the apostasy, the apostle includes "malicious gossips." This is the exact same word translated "devil" in John 6:70.

Perhaps you know people who always have something negative to say about others, always bringing negative information about people into their conversations. I'm praying that the Holy Spirit will reveal to us how "malicious gossip" is akin to the nature of Satan himself!

The Scriptures say that we will be justified or condemned by our words. Yes, our words, even those spoken in secret with a spouse or friend about others, are used by God to measure our obedience to His will. James writes, "If anyone does not stumble in what he says, he is a perfect man" (James 3:2).

Words have power. Scripture reveals that "Death and life are in the power of the tongue" (Prov. 18:21). Our words, expressed as a confession of faith, brought us into salvation; but words without faith can lead us and others with us into destruction and heartache.

James 3:8 warns, "the tongue . . . is a restless evil and full of deadly poison." "The tongue," he says, "is a fire, the very world of iniquity" (v 6). Listen carefully as James reveals a most profound thought. He says that the "tongue . . . sets on fire the course of our life, and is set on fire by hell" (v 6).

Satan gains access to our world, to destroy all that is good and holy in it, through our tongues! The very course of our life, the direction and quality of our earthly existence, is "set on fire by hell" through the words we speak! If we talk negatively about someone or maliciously gossip, the destructive fire of hell itself is released through our words! Lord, help us to understand the power of our words!

I believe God wants to break the power of gossip and negative speaking from the church! We may have a perfect analysis of what is wrong and why it is evil, yet if all we do is talk about it, we have yet to disavow our allegiance to hell. God calls us to be a house of prayer for all nations—a spiritual community that is mature, fully capable of seeing what is wrong, but positioning itself to release redemption into the world.

IF PAUL VISITED YOUR COMMUNITY

Imagine if the apostle Paul came into a typical American city. Do you know what he might say about our divisions? Probably what he told the Corinthians, "I am afraid that perhaps when I come . . . there may be strife, jealousy, angry tempers, disputes, slanders, gossip" (2 Cor 12:20).

Does that remind you of any churches any-where? Strife? Jealousy? Slanders and gossip? How can we approach God with these things existing in us? I believe God desires to give the church a whole new approach. However, we cannot lay hold of the future unless we first let go of the past.

Perhaps you are thinking, "So and so should hear this." Yes, but my hope is that we will start with ourselves. Pastors must stop talking negatively about people; they need to refrain from "leaking" problems with people into their sermons; interces-sors must stop negative gossip about the people they should be praying for. If we discuss what is wrong for ten minutes, let us pray for redemption for twenty.

JUDGE NOT

How do you respond to life's imperfections? Do you gossip? When you hear of someone's fail-ure, are you quick to spread the news? If Jesus was looking at the Christians with whom you fellow-ship, would He say to you what He spoke to His early apostles, that "one of you is a malicious gos-sip?"

Even if you are not a gossip or slanderer, you must be careful to avoid "fellowship" with gossips. Criticisms incubate. Paul warned that "a little leaven leavens the whole lump" (1 Cor 5:6). If we walk with the wise, we'll become wise, but if we open our heart to the cynical and critical, we, in fact, become like them. That is why Jesus said we were to "take heed" what we listened to. For what-ever we intently focus upon, we absorb in abun-dance (see Mark 4:24).

Thus, we must not even listen to gossip. When God shows us what is wrong in life, it is so we can pray for redemption, not spread the bad news all over town. Prayer has a very positive focus. People with Christ's love have a spiritual vision that causes them to see beyond the imperfections and limitations of the present world into the potential awaiting in the future—and they pray until what they see comes to pass.

Remember, none of us stands perfectly upright. Every time we judge someone, we position ourselves to be judged as well. Indeed, we each continually lean in the direction of our weakness. Only by the grace of God are we kept from falling. The moment we begin to self-righteously judge or gossip about another for their failings, we lean a little closer toward our own fall.

Let our actions and words be motivated by mercy. If we must discuss the situation or individual, let us harbor no malice or ill will. Let redemption be our guide, not revenge. Let us keep ourselves from becoming those who betray the working of Christ on the earth. Let us keep ourselves from the realm of the malicious gossip.

Declare War on Grumbling

God destroyed Israel for its grumbling, murmuring and complaining against Moses. Rarely is there a church split or division that does not have, as one of its roots, a grumbling element in the church. Earlier, we mentioned that, when Jesus referred to Judas Iscariot as a "devil," He was referring to the generic, impersonal definition of the word *diabolos* which meant "slanderer" or "malicious gossip." Judas evidently could not keep his negative perspective to himself.

Indeed, it isn't hard to imagine that, before Judas betrayed Christ, he expressed many criticisms of Jesus to the Pharisees—the final offense being that Jesus allowed a very expensive ointment to be "wasted" by being poured upon His head (see Matt 26:7). "Why was this perfume not sold for three hundred denarii, and given to poor people?" Judas asked indignantly (John 12:5).

His attitude actually led a minor insurrection toward Jesus, causing indignation to spread among the other apostles as well (see Matt 26:8). Who permitted this thoughtless luxury? Jesus did. Who reaped its immediate benefits? Again, the answer is Jesus. Perhaps, in Judas' critical mind, the last straw before betraying Jesus was that He did not apologize for this apparent "misuse of funds," but instead defended her extravagant act.

Betrayal is never a sudden thing; rather, it is an accumulative response to the unresolved anger, disappointment or jealousy one feels toward another. The offenses we do not transfer to God in surrendered prayer inevitably decay and become a poison within our spirits. This poison is then transferred to others through slander. We feel justified, yet we have actually become malicious gossips. We feel we are only serving the cause of "truth," when, in fact, we've become enemies to the cause of love.

A PROBLEM WITH GRUMBLING

To understand the betrayal of Christ, however, we must descend into its source: a grumbling spirit. When we lose sight of the many things for which we should be thankful, we become murmurers and grumblers, increasingly absorbed with a thought-life born in hell. Remember, Lucifer found fault with God in heaven! Paradise is not even enough for a grumbling spirit!

Beware when your anger toward another Christian has led you to gossip about him, especially if he's a church leader. Yes, beware: for you are no longer being conformed to Christ, but to the one who delivered Him up.

Of course, this grumbling attitude was not isolated to Judas. Many would-be disciples and Jewish leaders were also infected with it. Consider: there were miracles everywhere, and Christ had just fed the 5,000, yet a large crowd began to find fault.

"Do not grumble among yourselves," Jesus warned (John 6:43). Yet, they persisted. Remember, these were not just people who did not know Christ, but His very disciples, and they were not grumbling at a sinner, but the only sinless man who ever lived. Again, we read, "But Jesus, conscious that His disciples grumbled at this, said to them, 'Does this cause you to stumble?' " (John 6:61). Yet, still the grumbling spirit continued, until "many of His disciples withdrew, and were not walking with Him anymore" (John 6:66).

Grumbling caused people to stop seeing miracles, become offended by Christ's words, and stop walking with Him. As it was then, so it is today. Grumbling will ultimately cause you to stop walking with Jesus. It is a killer. Incredibly, the early disciples (not just the Pharisees) found fault with the Son of God! They had heaven in their midst and couldn't see it. That's what a grumbling attitude can do.

This poison is prevalent in the church today. I tell you plainly: God doesn't want a grumbling people to represent Him on earth. If we are habitually gossiping, grumbling or complaining, we should beware: the path we are on leads away from Christ.

THE THANKFUL HEART

Personally, I've declared war on grumbling. I've declared an unthankful heart is an enemy to God's will. Can you join me with this? Can you crucify a murmuring spirit? We have received too much from God to allow ourselves opportunities for unbelief. We have received too many gifts and privileges to allow a grumbling, murmuring heart to disqualify us from our destiny.

In contrast, the thankful heart sees the best part of every situation. It sees problems and weaknesses as opportunities, struggles as refining tools, and sinners as saints in progress. My prayer, dear ones, is for each of us to possess the abundant life that Jesus came to give us. I want to wrestle that little, ugly grumbling thing off your soul and put a living awareness of the goodness of God in its place!

The very quality of our lives decays as we murmur. Paul warned, "Nor let us . . . grumble, as [Israel] did, and were destroyed by the destroyer" (1 Cor 10:9,10). Every time we open ourselves to grumbling, our lives open up to destruction.

Again, Paul wrote, "Whatever is true, whatever is honorable . . . right, whatever is pure . . . lovely . . . if there is any excellence and if anything worthy of praise, let your mind dwell on these things" (Phil 4:8).

If your mind is fixed on something other than the wonderful life of God, it's not "fixed," it's broken. God wants to give us a new attitude. You say, "Who's going to take care of finding all the things that are wrong?" Oh, there are plenty of volunteers for that. Better to ask, "How can I attain the blessed life Jesus came to give me?"

A Blessed Family and Future

We must learn to be thankful for the people God has given us. Some of you cannot communicate with your loved ones. Why? Part of the reason is that we are unappreciative of them. You see, just as God requires we "enter His gates with thanksgiving" (Ps 100:4), so we gain access and the "right to speak" into the hearts of our loved ones through genuinely appreciating the good things we see within them.

For example, if you're not thankful for your teenagers, your disappointment with them will ultimately drive them from you. Take time with them and sincerely communicate the things you appreciate about them. There are many good things

about them that they need to hear you acknowledge. I am not saying we shouldn't correct our children, but that we must balance correction with
appreciation and praise, reinforcing their sense of
self worth and value.

Because God has created us to be social crea-
tures, we are born with an inner desire for acceptance. In fact, we desire acceptance more than we
seek for righteousness. By appreciating our loved
ones, we affirm and settle the search for acceptance that compels them toward ungodly associa-
tions. Just as when property "appreciates,"
increasing in value, so when we appreciate our
loved ones, destructive tendencies created by self-
hatred and fear of rejection are removed. We inspire them to become better, not by continually
harping on what's wrong with them, but by clearly
appreciating and establishing what is right.

There's something like radar inside the human
heart that senses the displeasure of others. Displeasure and ingratitude are like a repellant to human relationships. People think, "If I can't measure
up, if you can't see anything good in me, I'll go
where people will accept me as I am." Thanksgiving brings our loved ones closer to us rather than
driving them away.

Speaking of the people the Father put in His
life, Jesus prayed, "Thine they were, and thou
gavest them me" (John 17:6 KJV). One translation
reads, "They are your gift to me" (NAB). Jesus didn't
think of His disciples as always falling short, or as
a hindrance; rather, He welcomed them into His
life as a gift of His Father's love. Did they fail Him?
Yes. But He was thankful and treated them with
reverence and gratitude.

Your loved ones, your pastor and your church
are gifts from God. Tell them you appreciate them.
Personally, I am deeply thankful to God for my
wife and her love and support. Likewise, I thank
God for my children and the people I serve at my

church; our pastors, elders and deacons are wonderful people. Are any of them perfect? No, but I appreciate them as gifts from the hand of God Himself.

However, I know married couples who, every time they talk intimately, continually wind up discussing what's wrong with their relationship. Why not stop talking about it and just do what's right? Do you understand? Ingratitude is "relationship repellent." Thanksgiving, on the other hand, is the doorway to oneness.

Truly, we ought to be the happiest, most joyful, earthshaking individuals the world has ever seen. God is for us. He's written our names in the Book of Life. That alone is more than enough to make us invincibly thankful, happy, glad and joyful.

Some of you have been gossiping and grumbling. It's time for a fast. From what? From grumbling. For the next thirty days, each time you're tempted to complain, find something for which to be thankful. Make lists of people and things that you are thankful to God for. Let's put an end to grumbling and complaining and become a people who possess the wonderful life of God!

Let's pray: *Lord, deliver me from words that carry gossip. Master, I realize that I, too, at times have betrayed You when I gossiped and grumbled about other Christians. Jesus, create in me a passion to walk in thanksgiving and praise to You. Free me to be an encourager to others. Amen.*

—FROM THE BOOK, *IT'S TIME TO END CHURCH SPLITS*

SELF TEST, CHAPTER NINE
Remember, we are looking for answers that correspond with this training. Please write out your essay answers, allowing the Holy Spirit to provoke your thoughts. You may want to use them for group discussion. Note: we do not provide answers to essay questions. To check your multiple choice answers, see answer key in the next session.

Chapter 9, Essay #1: What does the Word say about gossip?

Chapter 9, Essay #2: What are some ways I can develop a thankful heart in order to declare war on grumbling?

1. Satan gains access to our world:
    a. in our prophetic dreams
    b. through our tongues
    c. through our journals
    d. in our prayers

2. God measures our obedience to His will by:
    a. our words
    b. our style of worship
    c. our work
    d. our diet

3. Whatever we intently focus upon, we absorb in abundance. Therefore what can we conclude about gossip?
    a. focus on gossip keeps us close to the Lord
    b. gossip is acceptable when the focus is in secret with a spouse or friend
    c. if we walk with gossips, we'll become wise
    d. take heed what we listen to; avoid fellowship with gossips

4. Betrayal is an accumulative response to:
    a. offenses we don't transfer to God in surrendered prayer
    b. unresolved anger, disappointment or jealousy one feels toward another
    c. truth and love
    d. both a & b

5. What is the new attitude God wants to give us that declares war on grumbling?
    a. vengeance
    b. righteous anger
    c. a thankful heart
    d. all the above

6. How does it affect someone when we clearly appreciate and establish what is right in them?
    a. causes them to become prideful
    b. we inspire them to become better
    c. destructive tendencies are removed
    d. both b & c

7. _____ is the doorway to oneness.
   a. Thanksgiving
   b. Talking about what's wrong
   c. Seeing where our loved ones fall short of our expectations
   d. all the above

8. What could you do to "fast from grumbling?"
   a. each time you're tempted to complain, find something for which to be thankful
   b. focus on what needs to change in your relationships
   c. make lists of people and things you are thankful to God for
   d. both a & c

QUOTE:

"We may have a perfect analysis of what is wrong and why it is evil, yet if all we do is talk about it, we have yet to disavow our allegiance to hell. God calls us to be a house of prayer for all nations—a spiritual community that is mature, fully capable of seeing what is wrong, but positioning itself to release redemption into the world."

SESSION SIX:

OUR GIFT TO CHRIST

CHAPTER TEN

BECOMING THE ANSWER TO CHRIST'S PRAYER

"Show me in the Bible," the pastor urged, "Show me where God says our different churches are supposed to be united."

I tried to restrain myself but it wasn't easy. I didn't want to overwhelm him with the hundreds of Scriptures that call us, either directly or indirectly, to unity with other born-again Christians.

I had heard his complaint before. In the theology of my new acquaintance, to say, "Okay, I'll unite in prayer with other pastors," was tantamount to saying, "Yes, I'll join the One World Church and follow the Antichrist." In his mind, any unity with other churches was blatantly false; it meant closing his eyes and being swallowed up in the "great falling away."

I took a breath. Long ago I realized that, often, when people study the Bible, instead of believing what they read, they only read what they already believe. Not only did I need just the right text, I also needed the wisdom and gentleness of Christ.

Should I use the book of Romans, where Paul provided a variety of ways to bring Jewish and Gentile Christians into unity? (Rom 3:22b–23; 3:29;

4:16–17; 5:16–19; 6:5; 12, 14 and 16). Or should I reference First and Second Corinthians, where Paul rebukes Christians for their divisions (1 Cor 1:10–13; 3:1–4, 21–23; 2 Cor 12:20–21), while also calling the church to their highest diversity and harmony (1 Cor 12–14)?

So much of the New Testament is given to the subject of unity that it was difficult to decide. I didn't have much time, so I went right to John 17, which not only talks about the unity of Christians, but reveals the heart of Christ as He Himself pleads for unity.

"Do you think the Scripture is true," I asked, "that 'Jesus Christ is the same yesterday and today, yes and forever'?" (Heb 13:8) He answered affirmatively. "And, would it be safe to imagine, since Jesus ever lives to make intercession for the church, that He would be praying for the same things today that He asked for in the first century?" (see Rom 8:27; Heb 7:25) Again he agreed. I then asked him to turn to the gospel of John.

To truly study Jesus' prayer in John 17, in my opinion, is to step into His heart. Here we discover how Jesus views people who are united as His followers, but are divided by their own fears, ambitions, and world views.

Besides the wide disparity of their doctrinal and social origins, Jesus' disciples were known to argue about their position. They were frequently subject to carnal ideas and hidden agendas, often not realizing in the least what Jesus meant when He taught. One, Matthew, was a former "IRS agent." Several were simple, uneducated, blue collar workers—mere fishermen; James and John were former "Baptists" who church hopped to the Jesus Movement; and two, Simeon the Zealot and Judas Iscariot were right-wing nationalists, the social equivalent of the Montana Freeman.

No wonder Jesus was praying for them to be one!

Christ's disciples were divided along many lines, yet Jesus did not sanction their divisions or pretend those divisions did not exist. Jesus didn't lower His expectations to the carnality of His disciples. Instead He prayed for their standards to be raised to the oneness of the Godhead!

The Spirit of Christ who dwells within us is pleading for our unity. How can we be so deaf to His desires, so cold toward His passions? How can we say we love Him and not keep His commandments or embrace His vision for us?

It is Satan who seeks to take our focus off Jesus. The devil manipulates our natural and cultural distinctions and turns them into reasons to divide from other born-again Christians. The issues that divide born-again Christians are not really our conflicts, but part of the larger conflict between Satan and the Lord Jesus. The devil can't touch the Lord directly, but he can exploit our divisions to bring pain to the heart of Christ.

We must see that, as much as we think we are defending the truth, to continue in our carnal divisions is actually to reinforce the deceptions of the devil himself.

It is amazing to me how Satan has convinced so many born-again Christians that unity with other believers is evil! If there ever was a false doctrine that was so widespread, so accepted in the body of Christ, yet so contrary to the heart and teachings of Christ, it is the tradition of division within the church!

Of course, my minister friend is correct not to unite with every so-called Christian or church organization. There are many false Christians; Satan still masquerades as an angel of light. Yet, in my opinion, the question is not whether we will be led astray and become false; the challenge today is whether we will repent of the unbiblical divisions among born-again Christians and finally become true!

The Source of True Unity

Upon what basis should we build unity? In John 17 Jesus gave us three dynamics, three fundamental truths which He said would lead His church into the most profound state of unity, such as the Father and Son enjoyed. That state of oneness would be accessed by our correctly relating to His name, His Word, and His glory.

First, here's what He prayed concerning the oneness produced by His name. He said, "Holy Father, keep them in Thy name, the name which Thou hast given Me, that they may be one, even as We are" (John 17:11).

God calls us into unity with all those who, like us, have called upon the name of the Lord. This is a wide umbrella and the unity here is not based on common interpretation of doctrinal positions, but on a common need of God's help and forgiveness. The fact is, we are already united under the redemptive power of Christ's name. This is not something to attain, but to acknowledge and accept, for at the foot of His cross, we are one.

But if the name of Jesus has given us a positional oneness, the words of Jesus bring us into functional oneness. Here again Jesus defined the conditions that create oneness. He prayed,

> I do not ask in behalf of these alone, but for those also who believe in Me through their word; that they may all be one; even as Thou, Father, art in Me, and I in Thee, that they also may be in Us; that the world may believe that Thou didst send Me.
> —John 17:20–21

When Jesus prays for unity in His church, He does not make the source of that unity man's innate ability to organize himself around projects or ideals; He says that it is through the "word, that they may all be one."

When Christ refers to "their word," He is actually speaking of the testimony of two things. The first proclaims what Jesus did, thus establishing the redemption mission in all who believe. And then it speaks of the continuation and replication of what Jesus said, which creates oneness in the lives of those who now follow. This was the very heart of the Great Commission (see Matt 28:20).

Christ's life, as it is embodied in both His redemptive mission and His teaching, is the foundational reality upon which all of Christianity is constructed. His sacrifice atones for our past; His Word establishes and creates our future. It is here that true oneness and Christian discipleship emerge.

He has given us His name and His Word, both of which create and establish oneness in the church. But the last stage of unity is the highest and most wonderful. For into hearts prepared by the Word He descends in the living splendor of His Presence. He said,

> And the glory which Thou hast given Me
> I have given to them; that they may be one,
> just as We are one; I in them, and Thou in
> Me, that they may be perfected in unity,
> that the world may know that Thou didst
> send Me, and didst love them, even as
> Thou didst love Me.   —John 17:22–23

"I in them, and Thou in Me, that they may be perfected in unity" (Gk. "Into a unit"). This is the height and goal of true Christianity: the revelation of Jesus Christ through His church. We receive provisional oneness through His name, functional oneness created and maintained through Christ's Word; and the awe of a living oneness produced by Christ's indwelling glory. This is not something that will only happen in the sweet by and by, but something that is so explicitly here that even "the world" may come to "believe."

WE CAN ANSWER HIS PRAYER

Jesus is the one answer I seek for all my prayers. If I ask for guidance, He is my Shepherd; if I am sick, He is my Healer. When I am perplexed, He is my Teacher. But there is something we can give back to our wonderful Savior. We can be the answer to His prayer for unity.

Each time we choose to pray for others, instead of criticize, we are answering His prayer. Every time we turn and forgive a brother who has hurt us, we are answering His longing. When we unite with other churches across racial or denominational lines; when we give ourselves in love, in prayer, in good deeds, in humble and joyful service to stand with God's people regardless of their background, we are actually increasing the pleasure in Christ's heart.

Think of it. As small and otherwise ordinary as we are, we can be the answer to His prayer, *Father make them one.*

Let's pray: *Dear Jesus, I want to be an answer to Your prayer. Help me to access oneness with You by correctly relating to Your name, Your Word, and Your glory. Then use me as an instrument of Your love to unite Your church.*

—FROM THE *ICIT* WEEKLY MAILER

SELF TEST, CHAPTER TEN

Remember, we are looking for answers that correspond with this training. Please write out your essay answers, allowing the Holy Spirit to provoke your thoughts. You may want to use them for group discussion. Note: we do not provide answers to essay questions. To check your multiple choice answers, see answer key at end of this session.

Chapter 10, Essay #1: When Christ refers to "their word" in John 17:20–21, He is actually speaking of the testimony of two things. They are:

Chapter 10, Essay #2: How can we answer the prayer of Jesus in John 17?

1. What does Jesus' prayer in John 17 reveal about His heart's desire among Christians?
   a. His desire that they be quickly united in heaven
   b. He desires they be separated from the world
   c. He pleads for unity
   d. His passion is for groups of similar spirituality

2. The disciples' doctrinal and social origins were:
   a. of wide disparity
   b. harmonious
   c. synonymous
   d. identical

3. The issues that divide born-again Christians are not really our conflicts, _____.
   a. but our pastors'
   b. but part of the larger conflict between Satan and the Lord Jesus
   c. but conflict that the world brings upon us
   d. but the elders' conflicts

4. What is the challenge today concerning unbiblical divisions?
   a. whether or not we will repent
   b. to plant new churches faster before division sets in
   c. to keep our worship styles consistent
   d. caution to not be led astray by following false Christians

5. What are the three fundamental truths upon which we build unity?
   a. gather, then divide and conquer
   b. we must build, stand and unite within the four walls of the church
   c. His name, His Word, and His glory
   d. the dust, the earth, then upon the rock

6. Being united with all those who have called upon "the name of the Lord" is based on:
   a. common interpretation of doctrinal positions
   b. a common need of God's help and forgiveness
   c. sticking together with your own denomination
   d. knowing the beliefs of your denomination

7. What is the height and goal of true Christianity?
   a. getting to heaven
   b. doing good deeds
   c. serving in the church
   d. the revelation of Jesus Christ through His church

8. What can happen through the awe of the living oneness produced by Christ's indwelling glory?
   a. "the world" may come to believe
   b. division
   c. judgment
   d. martyrdom

ANSWER KEY TO THIS SESSION'S
SELF TEST QUESTIONS:

CHAPTER TEN. Becoming the Answer to Christ's Prayer
1.c, 2.a, 3.b, 4.a, 5.c, 6.b, 7.d, 8.a.

ONLINE RESOURCES FOR
IN CHRIST'S IMAGE TRAINING

ONLINE SCHOOL INFORMATION

ICIT online school was established to empower individuals seeking greater conformity to Christ. Students from around the world register online and then receive two written messages each week via email. They also receive a set of 39 audio teachings (on 24 CDs or cassettes), which complement the written messages and add to the training. Students are then tested every six weeks and receive a cumulative grade at the end of six months; they also receive Level I certification from In Christ's Image Training.

The text materials used by our online school have been upgraded and reproduced into these four Level I manuals. If you are interested in continuing your studies, or if you desire certification through *In Christ's Image Training,* you will need to purchase and study the audio messages that accompany these manuals (see the following resource pages). You will then need to take a separate exam that will confirm to us that you have understood the training materials and are, indeed, pursuing the character of Christ.

For more information about current prices, special offers and the benefits of *In Christ's Image Training,* visit our web site at www.ICITC.org. No one will be refused training due to lack of funds.

CURRICULUM PACKAGE OPTIONS

LEVEL I BASIC TRAINING
(using Arrow Publications materials)
In Basic Training, the student/group studies at their own pace.

Full course: manuals and audio messages	$172.00
Manuals only (four books: Christlikeness, Humility, Prayer, Unity)	$52.00
Audio only (24 CDs or tapes)	$120.00

Materials available: Four manuals and 39 audio messages
(see back of Unity book for session and audio titles)

*Note: If you purchased this Basic Training package, you can still later enroll in the online school. To officially complete Level I and receive ICIT certification, you must enroll in our online school and successfully pass the final exam, after studying all manuals and audio teachings. Tuition cost for completion of Level I is $68.00. Visit www.ICITC.org for Level II tuition fees.

LEVEL I PREMIUM PACKAGE
(Enrollment in *ICIT* Online School)

When enrolled in ICIT Level I Online School, the commitment is for six months of training via weekly email lessons. Testing will be done every six weeks, following the completion of each track (Christlikeness, Humility, Prayer, Unity).

Individual Tuition	$240.00
Married Couple	$350.00
Group rate (per person, in group of six or more)	$85.00

Materials provided:
Sessions introduced through weekly email
39 audio messages on 24 CDs or tapes (included in tuition)

Benefits of Enrollment in *ICIT* Level I Online School:
Interaction with *ICIT* school and other *ICIT* students
Invitation to annual On-site Impartation Seminar
Certification with *In Christ's Image Training*
Diploma signed by Francis Frangipane
Opportunity to advance to Level II training
Opportunity to advance to Level III training
Opportunity to join Association of Pastors, Leaders, and Intercessors

For more information visit www.ICITC.org.

*NOTE:As an ICIT Level I online student, you are entitled to purchase one set of study manuals at a 50% discount, $26.00, from Arrow Publications.

ICIT MEMBER CHURCHES/ORGANIZATIONS

ICIT member churches/organizations may receive substantial discounts or other benefits for your church or organization when you purchase ICIT materials through Arrow Publications. For the most current offers and news, visit www.ICITC.org.

DISCIPLESHIP TRAINING BOOKLETS

$3.95 EACH (10+ AT 40%, 100+ AT 50% DISCOUNT)

COMPILED/FORMATTED FOR GROUP STUDY BY FRANCIS FRANGIPANE

A TIME TO SEEK GOD   #FF1-020 $3.95

DISCERNING OF SPIRITS *BESTSELLER!*   #FF1-018 $3.95

THE JEZEBEL SPIRIT *BESTSELLER!*   #FF1-019 $3.95

EXPOSING THE ACCUSER OF THE
   BRETHREN *BESTSELLER!*   #FF1-017 $3.95

PREVAILING PRAYER   #FF1-011 $3.95

REPAIRERS OF THE BREACH   #FF1-013 $3.95

DELIVERANCE FROM PMS   #DF1-002 $3.95

OVERCOMING FEAR!   #DF1-003 $3.95
     BY DENISE FRANGIPANE

TAPE ALBUMS

TAPE OF THE MONTH ANNUAL SUBSCRIPTION IS $54.50 (INCLUDING S&H)

TO KNOW GOD   #1FF5-032 4 tapes $20.00

IN HOLY FEAR   #1FF5-036 5 tapes $25.00

PRAYER WARRIOR   #1FF5-034 3 tapes $15.00

ON THE ARMS OF OUR BELOVED
     #1FF5-037 5 tapes $25.00

RECOMMENDED READING AND SELECTED CLASSICS

EVANGELISM BY FIRE
   by Reinhard Bonnke   #RB1-001 retail $15.00

INTERCESSORY PRAYER
   by Dutch Sheets   #DS1-001 retail $12.99

THE PROPHETIC MINISTRY
   by Rick Joyner   #RJ1-001 retail $12.99

YES, LORD! (LEARNING COVENANT THROUGH
MARRIAGE) by Sherry Thornton   #ST1-001 retail $12.00

FULL LIFE IN CHRIST (formerly LIKE CHRIST)
   by Andrew Murray   #AM1-001 retail $10.99

WAITING ON GOD
   by Andrew Murray   #AM1-002 retail $6.99

CHANGED INTO HIS LIKENESS
   by Watchman Nee   #WN1-001 retail $6.99

SIT, WALK, STAND
   by Watchman Nee   #WN1-002 retail $4.99

THE GREAT DIVORCE
   by C.S. Lewis   #CSL1-001 retail $9.95

PRACTICE OF THE PRESENCE OF GOD
   by Brother Lawrence   #BL1-001 retail $4.99

CO-PUBLISHED BY ARROW PUBLICATIONS

BREAKING CHRISTIAN CURSES: FINDING
   FREEDOM FROM DESTRUCTIVE PRAYERS
     #DC1-001 retail $15.00

YOU CAN ALL PROPHESY   #DC1-002 retail $10.00

THE NEXT 100 YEARS   #DC1-003 retail $12.00

     BY DENNIS CRAMER

JOURNAL OF THE UNKNOWN PROPHET
   by Wendy Alec   #WA1-001 retail $18.00 our price $16.00

THE BIRTH OF YOUR DESTINY
   by Victoria Boyson   #VBI1-001 retail $12.95 our price $10.95

FALLING TO HEAVEN
   by Mickey Robinson   #MR1-001 retail $12.00

HELP! I'M STUCK WITH THESE PEOPLE FOR
   THE REST OF ETERNITY!   *New!*
   by Susan Gaddis   #SG1-001 retail $12.00

Session and Audio Titles for Four Manuals

Track One: Christlikeness

Manual

Session One. The Vision: Becoming Christlike
Session Two. The Preeminence of Christ's Words
Session Three. The Eschatology of Christ's Fullness
Session Four. Revealing Christ in Suffering
Session Five. Victory in Warfare
Session Six. The Triumph of Christ's Life

Audio

#1a   Personal Welcome from Francis
#1b   Our Goal is Christ
#2a   God's Power in a Holy Life
#2b   More of God (part 1)
#3a   Hopelessness or Vision
#3b   With Unveiled Face
#4a   The Gift of Woundedness
#4b   The Perfection of Love
#5a   The Stronghold of Christ
#5b   Proven by Adversity
#6a   The Foundation of Christlikeness
#6b   Unoffendable

Track Two: Humility

Manual

Session One. Humility: The Virtue that Attracts God's Transforming Grace
Session Two. Those Whom God Chooses
Session Three. The Enemy of Grace: Religious Pride
Session Four. The Sacrifices of God: A Broken and Contrite Heart
Session Five. Becoming a Dwelling Place for God
Session Six. Humility: Flexible in Service to the Holy Spirit

Audio

#1a   Discovering Your Need
#1b   Blessed Are Those Who Mourn
#2a   Blessed are the Meek
#2b   Those Who Hunger
#3a   Blessed are the Merciful
#3b   They Shall See God
#4a   Peacemakers
#4b   The Prophets Before You
#5a   Becoming More Humble Than I Planned (part 1)
#5b   Becoming More Humble Than I Planned (part 2)
#6a   Perfectly Weak
#6b   The Spirit of Grace

Track Three: Prayer

Manual
Session One: Nations Shall Come to Our Light
Session Two: Intercession and Protection for Our Families
Session Three: The Power of One
Session Four: The Word at War
Session Five: Prayer in Pursuit of God's Presence
Session Six: The Ultimate Vision; The Most Powerful Prayer

Audio
#1a Praying for America (part 1)
#1b Praying for America (part 2)
#2a The Value of Prayer
#2b When You Have Done All, Stand
#3a Can You Drink the Cup (part 1)
#3b Can You Drink the Cup (part 2)
#4a Crushed by God (part 1)
#4b Crushed by God (part 2)
#5a The Priority of His Passion (part 1)
#5b The Priority of His Passion (part 2)
#6a Awakening the Pleasure of God (part 1)
#6b Awakening the Pleasure of God (part 2)

Track Four: Unity

Manual
Session One: The Roots of Division
Session Two: The Potential of Unity
Session Three: Enemies of Oneness
Session Four: Understanding Authority
Session Five: The Enemy's Subtleties
Session Six: Our Gift to Christ

Audio
#1a Healing the Heart of God (part 1)
#1b Healing the Heart of God (part 2)
#2a Building the House of the Lord (part 1)
#2b Building the House of the Lord (part 2)
#3a How To Honor Others
#3b Repairers of the Breach
#4a The Freedom of Authority
#4b The Perfection of Submission
#5a Breaking the Spirit of Strife
#5b More of God (part 2)
#6a The Days of His Presence (part 1)
#6b The Days of His Presence (part 2)